W0246893

PENGUIN BOOKS

WHAT CAN I GIVE?

Srijan Pal Singh studied at the Indian Institute of Management, Ahmedabad, where he won a gold medal for the best all-rounder student and was the student-council head. He has worked with the Boston Consulting Group (BCG) in a Naxalite-affected region to establish a transparent public-distribution system using technology interventions. He was nominated as one of the Global Leaders of Tomorrow at the St. Gallen Symposium in Switzerland.

Srijan has actively travelled across rural India and participated in various international initiatives to study and evolve sustainable development systems. Many of his articles on sustainability and development have been published in reputed journals. Srijan has actively worked with Dr Kalam to promote better-quality education which inspires young minds.

WHAT CAN I GIVE?

Life Lessons from My Teacher,
A.P.J. ABDUL KALAM

SRIJAN PAL SINGH

PENGUIN BOOKS

An imprint of Penguin Random House

PENGUIN BOOKS

USA | Canada | UK | Ireland | Australia
New Zealand | India | South Africa | China | Singapore

Penguin Books is part of the Penguin Random House group of companies
whose addresses can be found at global.penguinrandomhouse.com

Published by Penguin Random House India Pvt. Ltd.
4th Floor, Capital Tower 1, MG Road,
Gurugram 122 002, Haryana, India

First published by Penguin Random House India 2016

ISBN 9780143334262

Typeset in Dante MT Std by Manipal Digital Systems, Manipal
Printed at Replika Press Pvt. Ltd, India

www.penguin.co.in

Contents

Contents

Acknowledgements

First and foremost, I would like to express my gratitude to Dr Kalam, who will always continue to inspire me and many millions like me across the world. It is his way of life that has motivated the creation of this book. He remains a beacon of hope for the citizens of India and the world; his life story is something today's youth should absorb, emulate and narrate to others.

A large portion of the thoughts expressed in this book are essentially extensions of dreams, imaginings, fears, ambitions, hopes and challenges of all the ordinary citizens who shared their vision with us. I thank them all.

I would like to thank Ms Sohini Mitra, Ms Trisha Bora and Ms Nimmy Chacko for their untiring effort in helping us with the editing and quality improvement of the content. I'd also like to thank Mr Gunjan Ahlawat for his excellent cover design, and Ms Piya Kapur for ensuring that the copies of the book reach the right channels at the right time.

I would also like to thank Ms Hemali Sodhi for her support.

Acknowledgements

Finally, my deepest regards to my parents and teachers for the values they instilled in me; they enabled me to work with Dr Kalam and learn from him at every step of our time together.

Srijan Pal Singh

Introduction

A young mind is like clay. It can be moulded into any shape desired by a master craftsman. A teacher is such an artist.

Greatness is not visible externally; it lies within. Blessed is the man who comes across a guru who can tap into one's iceberg of potential.

This story is about one such exemplary teacher who changed my life forever and showed me who I truly am.

This story narrates how my childhood hero turned into a real lifelong mentor. It is about the days, lessons and lives shared between two people—one, a fresh graduate in his mid-twenties and the other, a man thrice his age. This is the story of Dr A.P.J. Abdul Kalam and the lessons I learnt from him, from the wisdom that shone through in his conversations, lunches, dinners, travels, discussions and the occasional argument.

Many of the stories that I share here are everyday events, albeit with extraordinary and unconventional lessons hidden in them. And this is what made Dr Kalam a great guru; he could polish ordinary pebbles into pearls of wisdom and share them with the world.

Introduction

In 2002, when I was barely eighteen, an amazing piece of news was taking the entire nation by storm. A paperboy, who had failed to become a pilot and become a space scientist instead—a missile man, a nuclear researcher—was on the verge of becoming the eleventh President of the nation. It was one of those rare occasions in politics when the citizens—that too, almost unanimously—were thankful to the political leaders for taking such a great decision. The papers and television news channels were abuzz with the story of his humble origins, his lifestyle, his books, his food habits and, of course, his hairstyle! A man without any particular political affiliation and with no organizational support was making his way to the highest office of the nation.

William Shakespeare wrote, 'Some are born great, some achieve greatness and some have greatness thrust upon them.'

Dr Kalam fulfilled all three categories of greatness.

Despite his humble beginnings, Dr Kalam was born with greatness ingrained in him. He was a Muslim born in Rameswaram—considered one of the holiest of towns by Hindus—who went on to receive a Christian missionary education for a large part of his formative years, and his best friend was the son of a local Hindu priest. His dreams of flying high were nurtured by a school teacher, Sri Siva Subramaniam Iyer, in a country which was not politically independent yet. Few souls get to experience such diversity of society and religion, imbibing the unflinching hunger of impossible dreams—that too in their early years.

Dr Kalam was then refined in the fires of failure—be it the failure to become a fighter pilot as a young graduate or the failure of the first Satellite Launch Vehicle (SLV) in 1979.

And he learnt how to overcome failures through his undying effort and perseverance. The difference between Dr Kalam and a lot of us is not the lack of troubles or failures, but the fact that all his failures taught him how to navigate his way through life. He would embrace these failures, and it's those invaluable lessons that enabled him to make more formidable attempts the next time around. He wore his failures like badges, and he valued them as much as his successes; at no point was he embarrassed to speak of them. Dr Kalam had the courage to take the bull by its horns and that is what made him great.

Throughout his career as a scientist, Dr Kalam was managing the technological ascent of a country that was still struggling with its myriad prejudices and internal conflicts. It was only because he seemed to truly rise above these ingrained attitudes—a seemingly impossible task—and was respected in equal measure by all, that he was considered a great president.

In the finer form of Hindi, the language of my home state, Uttar Pradesh, there is a word for those who are loved by all—*sarvapriya*. And there is a word for those who rise and become so powerful that no rival can defeat them—*ajay*—a very popular name across the country.

But besides these two, there is another word—a more powerful one. *Ajatashatru*—a man so loved that he has no rivals. Dr A.P.J. Abdul Kalam was a rare Ajatashatru of our times. He was rarely criticized, and even when he was, he handled it with grace.

In September 2015, six weeks after his demise, I was in Chennai, interacting with a small group of children in a government school. I asked them, 'When you grow up, what would you like to become?' All of them spontaneously raised their hands and shouted in unison, 'Kalam!'

Bharat Ratna Dr A.P.J. Abdul Kalam is best known for the generations he has inspired—to dream, excel and rise. He has shown his countrymen that hard work, sincerity and talent *do* bear fruit in the long run, and the choices and efforts we make in our lifetime can transcend the odds that we are born with.

Once, during a visit to Australia, in 2012, a professor introduced Dr Kalam to the class, saying, 'Even in his eighties, for the youth of India he commands the respect of a sage and the charisma of a rock star.'

Of course, Dr Kalam had a soft spot for the youth. I remember him saying many a time, 'Up to the age of seventeen, the mind of a youth can be shaped. Beyond that it becomes difficult.' Hence, he dedicated a large part of his life, during his presidential rule and beyond it, trying to shape the minds of the Indian youth. He wanted them to have three traits—righteousness, creativity and courage. He even formulated an equation, which he called the Knowledge Equation, where knowledge is a sum of these three traits. He said, 'Knowledge makes you great.' In four simple words he had outlined the pathway to greatness; such was the simplicity of Dr Kalam.

Dr Kalam paid attention to the minutest details. He and I co-authored three books and worked on over a thousand speeches that he delivered. And he would insist on revisiting each sentence multiple times and refining it till he was satisfied. It was not uncommon for us to go through twenty drafts of any important speech. Yet, minutes before going up on stage he would often say, 'Srijan, what are the new things we are going to talk about in this lecture?' Always looking to improve, he was ever eager for the next version.

On stage, he would look at the audience, their faces and expressions, whether they were in the shade or under the sun, and then point to a stray group of children huddled in a corner of the hall, in an audience of grown-ups, and tell me, 'Add that poem in the speech for the children out there.' He was apolitical but he understood people and their needs better than any veteran politician.

He had a voracious appetite for knowledge. Libraries and reading rooms occupied half of his house at 10, Rajaji Marg. Books used to be scattered all over his bedroom and even in the garden. He never set out on a journey without a couple of books in his bag. I remember lifting his bag on the last day of his life—it was heavy. I said, 'Sir, your bag is getting heavier!' He replied, 'That is because I am reading more!'

For me, what distinguished Dr Kalam from everyone else was not just his knowledge but his sensitivity and humility. He always introduced people as friends—whether they were his secretaries, his driver, his gardener, his cook, the housekeepers, or even a stranger he had just met! Dr Kalam viewed the world as truly flat—there was no place for hierarchies and ranks.

He had the gift of empathy, and his memory, when it came to others' difficulties, was extraordinary; it's why he was so loved. If he came across anyone suffering from a cold, he would offer them medicine and hot soup. The next day he would unfailingly inquire after their health—'Are you repaired?' Irrespective of their reply, his reaction would be, 'Funny fellow you are!'

He had an attitude of gratitude. He felt highly indebted to all his gurus—right from his primary-school teacher, Sri Siva Subramaniam, who inspired him to fly, to Vikram Sarabhai, who introduced him to space technology. 'Thank you' and 'What can I do for you?' were perhaps his most commonly used phrases. At the end of every trip, he would always thank his driver and security officer and gift them a signed copy of one of his books. No wonder so many government vehicle drivers and security officers from other states came to Delhi and Rameswaram to pay him their last respects. Dr Kalam had cast his magic on them.

Dr Kalam had a lot of faith in the youth of the nation. He was so concerned about the country's welfare that he had spent the last two hours of his life discussing the threat terrorism posed and the dangers of a dysfunctional Parliament. Even in his final moments, he trusted that the youth, particularly his students, would come up with solutions for the issues ailing our nation. He was an eternal believer in the ignited minds of the new generation—which he considered the most powerful gift on earth.

I had the greatest fortune of working closely with this great soul, of travelling with this curious mind, and of spending a bulk of my life with this benevolent human. For people he was the Missile Man but for me he was the Smile Man. The world saw him as a space scientist who placed satellites that revolved around the earth. I saw him as a great spirit who gifted dreams to people—dreams, and the courage for the common man to go after those dreams. The world saw his actions, while I was lucky enough to have witnessed his emotional side as well. He was a scientist, a saint, a writer, a teacher, a poet and a philosopher—all rolled into a single entity of compassion and wisdom.

Let me take you on a wonderful journey—a journey through the lessons that I learnt from Dr Kalam.

1

First Impressions

In September 2008, I was in the second year of my MBA at the Indian Institute of Management (IIM), Ahmedabad, popularly called IIMA. IIMA, now considered India's premier institution for management studies, was established in 1961, under the mentorship of Dr Vikram Sarabhai—the person Dr Kalam considered his greatest guru, albeit in the completely different field of space science. And the grand library, which is the pride of the campus, is named after Dr Sarabhai.

I lived in Dorm 18, which was at the far end of the hostel block in the old campus. The old campus is a historic red-brick building, which has nurtured some of the best minds of the nation through the ages.

In our course, we had six terms in total, with three terms each year. Each term would last for about three months. While everyone studied the same subjects in their first year, in the second year students were allowed to choose freely from a buffet of courses. The courses ranged from traditional management to entrepreneurship, from long trips to the mountains for self-exploration, to courses on governance, politics and leadership.

In the middle of my second year, something special and unthinkable happened.

We had an opportunity to participate in a course called Globalizing Resurgent India through Innovation Transformation (GRIIT). And the co-faculty for this course was none other than Dr A.P.J. Abdul Kalam—the eleventh President of India. By then he had completed his five years in the Rashtrapati Bhavan, and it was a presidency that the entire nation was proud of.

For many of my classmates, Dr Kalam was a childhood hero. For the children growing up during that period, Dr Kalam had seemed like a man blessed with superhuman qualities. Not only was he a president we all loved and admired, his was a story that parents often told their children. For the common man he was a symbol of India's quest for self-reliance and a man's success against all odds.

News got around that Dr Kalam was going to teach at the college, and immediately the course was in heavy demand—like a new edition of a favourite superhero story. About a hundred students signed up for the course, all in the hope of getting tutored by Dr A.P.J. Abdul Kalam.

Being the general secretary of the student union and the student coordinator for this course, I had the privilege of accompanying my professor Dr Anil Gupta to the airport to welcome Dr Kalam that September.

The plan was to escort our honourable guest to the state guest house in an area called Dafnala, which was about a kilometre away from the airport. The director of IIMA, Professor Sameer Barua, was supposed to join us at the guest house directly. We had decided against taking Dr Kalam to the IIMA campus, as it was a good forty-five-minute drive from the airport and we did not want to tire him out with this unnecessary hassle. We wanted him to be well-rested for next day's class, which was scheduled to start at 8.45 a.m. and carry on till the evening.

When Dr Kalam arrived at the airport lounge, my professor introduced me to my childhood hero as a 'good student and council leader'. I couldn't say a thing—so awed was I on seeing Dr Kalam in front of me.

He looked at me and immediately asked, 'Are you a good fellow?' While I was still trying to decipher the question and work out a suitable response, he held his hand out towards me. I was in a daze when I shook hands with him. I had pictured this moment in my head so many times, but when it actually happened, it felt *so* surreal. He proceeded to ask me a few questions about the class, about my project and about what the students would like to hear from him. When the conversation ended, I bowed down to touch his feet, as was customary in the city of *tehzeeb*, Lucknow, the place where I grew up.

'You are a good fellow, it seems!' he commented in his typical manner.

Later, when I was working with him and spending the better part of my days with him, it became a habit, a ritual almost, for me to shake his hands first and then touch his feet. For the next six years, whenever there was an important occasion, be it a birthday or a festival or the beginning of a new project, or even if I was going through a difficult time—it didn't matter—I made sure he was a part of it. He became irreplaceable in my life.

It was always a pleasure talking to Dr Kalam. It could be a simple greeting or a heart to heart, depending on the occasion. He would first shake hands and say a one-liner: 'Are you a good fellow?' or 'Be a good son' or 'How are you doing today?'

Then I would touch his feet as we completed our little discussion. 'Do well in life,' he would say. This ritual and his blessings were an important element of my life, right till our final day together.

That day at the airport when Dr Kalam learnt that the director of IIMA, Professor Barua, would be coming to greet him personally at the state guest house, he immediately paused and instructed his personal staff, 'I will go to IIM right now.'

I did not quite comprehend then why he insisted on this. I thought that something had gone wrong and that was why he wanted to change the itinerary. Forty minutes later the convoy reached the college campus. We stopped at the Kasturbhai Lalbhai Management Development Centre, better known as KLM. It was the building where senior guests and visiting faculty stayed.

At KLM he met the director and when his reason for visiting the campus became clear, we were all left in awe. His logic was simple and incredibly profound.

He told the director, 'Whatever I may be outside these walls, within this institution, I am a professor and you are the director. I should come to meet you and not the other way around. Hence I have come here to give you my regards.'

There could not have been a better lesson in humility. In one stroke he had won over everyone at IIMA.

But this was just the beginning.

That evening he stayed on at the campus till midnight, talking to the students about their projects. His secretary reminded him once, 'Sir, it is late. You should go and rest.'

He replied, 'These fellows must have also stayed up late, working on their projects. I can surely spend one long evening with them. Right?'

I realized much later that it was not unusual for him to spend long nights with students—they were his assets, and teaching them was his passion. Even on 27 July 2015, he was planning to stay up with his students at IIM Shillong till at least 11 p.m., listening to them speak about their projects on carefully chosen topics.

I am truly blessed to have known him closely and to have learnt from him. I couldn't have been more thrilled when I started working with him in 2008. The bond that a teacher shares with his student was sacred to him, completely uncoloured by hierarchies. And it is this bond that ensures that the light of wisdom travels unhindered, and in its purest form, from a teacher to a learner.

2

Medals Come with Responsibilities

Throughout the rest of 2008, and till my graduation from IIMA in April 2009, I was in regular touch with Dr Kalam over email and the occasional phone call. We would discuss the topic that we had chosen for research during class—Providing Urban Amenities in Rural Areas (PURA).

All IIMA students dream of securing great jobs—usually in tier-one consulting firms or in investment banking companies. These are the plush jobs everyone hunts for, the sort you hear about in the media. These jobs are collectively called the Day Zero placements because these are the first companies that arrive on campus for recruitment (though why it's called Day Zero is still not clear!). Not more than 20 per cent of the entire batch gets these highly coveted jobs.

Let me give you a little perspective. The toughest year in the job market was 2009. The massive financial breakdown in the USA had affected the investment-banking industry so badly that campus pundits were wondering whether the industry would survive at all. Day Zero placements were plummeting to zero—investment-banking jobs had totally evaporated and consulting jobs were barely trickling in. I was lucky to get a job offer from the Boston Consulting Group (BCG), the company I had done my first summer internship at.

In 2009, luck favoured me again. The KVS Gold Medal is highly prized at IIMA. It is awarded to the best all-rounder of the graduating batch. The evaluation criteria include factors like academic achievement, leadership qualities and performance in sports. It was my good fortune that I was chosen for this award.

After receiving my degree, I contacted Dr Kalam once again. The final term had got over and I was keen to meet him and tell him about the medal that I had been awarded. I requested him for a meeting at his New Delhi residence so that I could show him my medal in person.

Within two hours, I received a reply.

Congratulations for your success. Please come. You are most welcome. Do coordinate with my friend Sheridon for the appointment.
Kalam

I was thrilled. I got an appointment with him the next week itself. I was to meet him on 11 May 2009, at 3 p.m.

This was my first visit to his house and I was a little nervous. Yes, he had been my professor, but that was on campus—a familiar territory. Now here I was, in a VVIP residence. I reached 10, Rajaji Marg at the appointed hour. It was located between the Prime Minister's house and the President's Estate.

I was escorted in by an armed guard who was standing at the front gate. The house was a white-coloured, two-storey structure, with a garden in front and one at the back. It was lined with trees, some of them unusually tall and others oddly spread out. Numerous birds flew about the garden, busy at work, barely noticing the presence of humans.

'Sir has asked you to meet him upstairs. Take these stairs and turn left. There is a library. He is sitting there,' his help told me.

While I was climbing up the stairs, my gold medal and my degree seemed to be weighing me down. It was almost five months since I had last met him. I wondered how this meeting would go. 'Does he even remember me?' This sudden doubt made me nervous.

Dr Kalam was sitting in front of a small table that was piled high with heavy books. The pile was precariously balanced. He was wearing a red T-shirt and a pair of trousers and held a book in his hand.

On seeing me, he said, 'Oh, you have come! Sit, sit.' I took the chair facing him.

'I am happy to know that my student has got a gold medal. You are a good fellow,' he said.

His open and sincere manner put me at ease.

Our conversation began with a recollection of our time in IIMA. I was happy and relieved that he remembered so many things from our classroom interaction. Then I decided to show him my degree and medal. This seemingly innocent, albeit slightly boastful activity was going to change me profoundly in the next few minutes.

I showed him my degree first. 'Sir, I got this degree for the PGP course.'

He took it from me and studied it. Next, I thrust the gold medal at him.

'And, sir, here's the medal,' I declared proudly.

He took that as well and observed them both closely. He then handed the degree scroll back to me and said, 'So . . . these are for your good marks, right?'

I nodded.

Then he held out the medal and asked, 'This is the gold medal. Is it really made of gold?'

I was caught off-guard for a moment. 'Yes, sir, it's 22-carat gold. That is why it is so small.' I thought that Dr Kalam was criticizing the size of the medal and I got defensive about it.

'The size of the medal might be small but the effort made to obtain it must have been huge. That is what matters,' he replied.

There was a moment of silence. He then leaned back on his chair, brought his hands together and said, 'So you have got a great degree with good marks.'

'Sure. Of course.'

'So we can assume that you've had the best education. You have also got a medal, that too a medal made of gold. So we can also assume that you have some intelligence and talent beyond academics.'

I nodded, trying to hold back my excitement. The president's appreciation was feeding my ego.

He continued, 'And I am sure that when you got the medal, you got public recognition too?'

'Yes, the award was presented to me in front of all the students, parents and faculty,' I confirmed.

'Very good,' he said, taking a moment to reflect. 'So, Srijan, you have been gifted with the best education, blessed with high intelligence and you have acquired the much sought-after golden recognition. Don't you think that it is now your responsibility to use all this not only for your own progress, but also for the progress of the nation and for solving the problems of the world? Wouldn't that be doing true justice to your abilities?'

These words struck me like a knife. I was shaken. I was there only to meet Dr Kalam, to show him the medal, to get his autograph and to get some pictures clicked with him. After that I was going to join BCG within the next three weeks.

But suddenly, I felt the gravitational pull of the responsibilities that had been bestowed on me along with my gold medal.

Dr Kalam continued, 'Srijan, let me tell you something from my own experience. Every talent has a responsibility. Each achievement comes with an expectation. Medals come with the weight of duty. Don't be scared . . . but be aware. Enjoy it, as duties only make you a bigger person. From now on, wherever you go, just remember that you have to live up to your award.'

As I took in his advice, I felt profoundly moved. Without much thought, I blurted out, 'I understand, sir. Can you teach me how to fulfil my duties, as you are also my teacher? Would you allow me to do a three-week internship with you so that I can further explore some topics that you taught us at IIMA? It will help me grow, and I promise my work will be of use to you.'

It was wishful, even impulsive, of me to ask—it had come out of the blue and neither of us was expecting it. But he did not try to bail out of it.

'I will let you know later today,' he said.

I shook his hand and touched his feet. I refrained from using my camera. Some moments in life are richer than what a lens can capture; they are best etched in memory than developed on a roll.

Later that day, Major General Swaminathan, his adviser, called from Dr Kalam's office and confirmed my internship. He did not mention the period of the internship, and I did not ask. I was supposed to report the next week. I did not know it then, but I was the first ever intern to work with him at 10, Rajaji Marg.

My life had changed. From a classroom teacher, Dr Kalam had become my personal mentor.

The internship, which was supposed to last three weeks, stretched on for two months. I started getting calls from BCG, as I had not joined them on the scheduled date. In such dynamic companies, a month's delay in joining can affect one's promotions and ratings hugely.

When the second month of my internship started, I finally summoned the courage to write a mail to the company's HR head, stating that I would not be joining them. This was something I had not discussed with anyone, not even my family, and not with Dr Kalam either. Nobody knew that I was leaving a cushy corporate job.

In retrospect, this was the best decision of my life.

By this time, around the end of July, I was enjoying all the challenges coming my way and was probably doing a decent job of tackling them. Dr Kalam asked me one day, 'Aren't your parents worried about what you are doing?' It was a valid question, and while I was blessed with rather 'cool' parents, I had caused some flutters, given that I also had a hefty student loan to clear. I nodded, saying, 'A little, but I will handle it.'

I was very pleasantly surprised at what he said next. 'Don't worry, I will visit them and tell them you are a good fellow.'

For a while I could not believe what he had said. I clarified, 'Okay, sir. I will ask them to come and meet you here.'

'No, don't be a funny guy. I am going to Lucknow next week and I will go meet them.'

On 3 August 2009, much to the surprise of my family, my neighbours and the Lucknow media, the ex-president of the country visited the modest home of his student. That was one of the greatest gifts he could ever have given me.

By November, I was staffed permanently with Dr Kalam, graduating from an intern to an Officer on Special Duty and Adviser to the former President of India. In another year, we would publish our first book together—*Target 3 Billion*. This association would hold strong till my teacher's last breath.

An Oath for the Youth by Dr A.P.J. Abdul Kalam

1. I will have a goal and work hard to achieve that goal. I realize that small aim is a crime.
2. I will work with integrity and succeed with integrity.
3. I will be a good member of my family, society, the nation and the world.
4. I will always try to save or better someone's life, without any discrimination of caste, creed, language, religion or state. Wherever I am, a thought will always come to my mind. That is, what can I give?

5. I will always protect and enhance the dignity of every human life without any bias.

6. I will always remember the importance of time. My motto will be 'Let not my winged days be spent in vain'.

7. I will always work for a clean planet and clean energy.

8. As a youth of my nation, I will work with courage to achieve success in all my tasks and enjoy the success of others.

9. I am as young as my faith and as old as my doubts. Hence, I will light the lamp of faith in my heart.

10. My national flag flies in my heart and I will bring glory to my nation.

3

Criticism Comes with a
Heavy Debt

During my early days with Dr Kalam, we established a custom that we carried on till the very end. We would discuss the daily news—whether we gathered it from the papers, magazines, books or the Internet. There was no topic under the sun that we wouldn't cover in our riveting conversations.

Every day, as soon as he would walk into the office, even before taking his seat, he would want to know about the news. 'So, funny guy, what's happening in the world?' This would be my cue to tell him about the news articles I had gathered for the day. Once I was done, he would say, 'I have something interesting for you too.' Then he would carefully pick up the pages that he had been perusing at bedtime, or in the morning, and read them out to me. This was how we came up with the content of the three books that we co-authored.

Back in 2010, one particular spiritual guru became the subject of national debate. The guru alleged that he had been fired at. The police, however, denied the incident, even as the guru claimed that it was an attempt on his life. Media frenzy followed, and the incident became a topic of popular discussion in no time. The police's version of the story made me doubt the guru.

So during one of our morning conversations, I criticized the guru at length for raising alarm so recklessly and argued that he was simply trying to garner sympathy. Dr Kalam listened to me patiently, putting forth a few questions every now and then, but he didn't dismiss my arguments right away.

Two weeks later, when we were at the dinner table at his house, he extended a printed article towards me and said, 'Read it. It might interest you. What do you think about this?'

The article was about the same guru whom I had criticized two weeks ago. It described how he was bringing faith and peace to thousands through his new methods of meditation and unity. So much so that his fame had reached over a hundred different countries.

My immediate response was to be defensive. 'Well, this might be true. But this is the same person whose allegations were refuted by the police—'

'When you are criticizing someone for doing something you believe is not appropriate, you take on the responsibility of wholeheartedly appreciating them for their achievements and that, with double the energy.'

He continued, 'When someone does something worthy of praise, don't let personal bitterness over past issues dilute the vigour of your appreciation for them. That would be unfair. Criticism is a debt, which needs to be paid off with applause. It takes a toll not only on the one who is being criticized but also on the one who is criticizing. Criticism should be given, and taken, wisely. Once you have criticized someone, ensure that you note down their name—you need to follow up on it and constantly assess if your criticism was correct. Be the first one to applaud them when they do something wonderful. Such should be the circle of criticism. You have to outweigh the debt of criticism with appreciation, whenever possible. Above all, it is very important to learn to enjoy the success of others.'

From that day on, I started keeping track of all my creditors—those I had criticized in any capacity—in the same diary where I noted down the lessons I learnt from Dr Kalam. Over time, I repaid my debts and the list kept getting shorter.

This was another important characteristic of Dr Kalam. He rarely criticized anyone. Even when he had negative feedback, he would offer it as a suggestion and not as criticism. That is a healthy thing to do, I have come to realize over the years, because the intent should be to help and not to hurt, not punish but correct. Pointing fingers is of no use to anyone; nudging people in the right direction is much better. Dr Kalam had never incurred the debt of criticism in his life.

As for enjoying the success of others, there is nothing better than expanding the circle of people whose happiness can make us happy. I have come to realize the depth and power of this simple principle.

If our happiness depends on our perception of events, then we should try to perceive every event in such a way that can bring us joy.

4

Hard Work Deserves the Greatest Respect

A hallmark of Dr Kalam's lifestyle was the 'Walk'.

The Walk almost always happened at 3 p.m. every day when he was in Delhi. It was a one-hour stroll around his residence at Rajaji Marg. Nothing could come in the way of this walk. If it rained, he would carry an umbrella. In the month of May, when the heat was unbearable, he would walk in the shade, wearing a T-shirt and a pair of light summer trousers. In the harsh winters, the T-shirt would be replaced by a sweater and a shawl. If anyone wanted to meet him at this hour, they would be invited to walk along with him. But come what may, the Walk would proceed at three every afternoon.

Often, he would me to accompany him on his walks. Those hours were meant for contemplation and reflection. In fact, many of the finest ideas for our books, speeches and assignments evolved during our rounds.

Of all our walks together, there is one that I remember particularly well.

The path that Dr Kalam used to walk on wound around the rose bushes, which our gardener, Kanchan, tended carefully. Almost all the rose plants growing on that stretch bore red roses. Dr Kalam loved the roses and was very concerned about their well-being. Every time the roses blossomed, Kanchan would get a special reward. Dr Kalam often referred to Kanchan as 'my expert friend who grows roses for all of us'.

In September 2011, we were writing the book *Target 3 Billion*. New ideas kept cropping up even as the manuscript neared completion, and we were striving to incorporate them in the upcoming book. One afternoon, as I was accompanying him on his walk, listening to his ideas, a copy of the manuscript held in my hands, he suddenly gestured to me to stop.

'Let us reverse our direction,' he said.

I didn't know why he'd changed his mind so suddenly, but when the President asks you to walk in the opposite direction, you do so without question. So we took an about turn.

The area is known to harbour a colony of ferocious monkeys, who have no fear of humans. They roam about freely in large troops. And, quite often, a handler is deployed with a trained langur to get rid of the monkeys.

Usually, we'd avoid walking into the patch that the monkeys inhabited, and would try and stick to the path that was guarded by the langur. But as I turned around, I could not spot a single monkey; there was just a friendly langur looking dully at us, lazing in the shade. So I asked Dr Kalam, 'Why did you change direction? There are no monkeys here!' I thought he'd seen something I might have missed.

'There is something else,' he said. 'Look carefully.' He pointed at a rose bush not far from us.

I trained my eyes on the roses, squinting in the blinding sunlight. But I couldn't spot anything unusual. 'There's nothing here, sir.'

'You did not see carefully. Look at that flower. There are some fellows sitting on it.'

This time I looked properly, and indeed there were two bees sitting on the flowers, gathering nectar.

He then said, 'Look, buddy, the honeybee is doing its work. It is collecting food for its family and also pollinating the flower in the process. It is helping two species at once. It is very important work, I say. It is the work of God.' He smiled.

I knew the science behind pollination, but I had never noticed the spirituality behind the process. In one stroke he had taken me to a space where science met spirituality, where the power of knowledge met the might of observation.

'Such busy fellows they are,' he continued. 'Very hard-working little fellows. The one who works hardest deserves the greatest respect. And so we must change our direction, so we can admire them and take care not to disturb their great work.'

I was touched by his attention to detail and by his sensitivity towards nature's work. The respect for work, no matter who's doing it, is a profound lesson I learnt from him.

As we completed a round, we passed by the flowers again. But the bees had moved on to other flowers. I requested Dr Kalam to pose in front of those flowers because I wanted to remember that moment forever.

5

What Will I Be Remembered For?

Dr Kalam often ended his speeches addressed to youngsters with one question: 'What would you like to be remembered for?' It was a powerful way of imbuing young students with energy and dreams. It inspired them to aspire, think and act.

The first time I encountered this Kalam hallmark was in 2008, when I was a student at IIMA. Dr Kalam did not stop with that one question, however; he went on to share with us a list of fifteen career options from which we could choose our answer. I am putting down some of them for you.

- Would you like to be remembered for pioneering action in interconnecting waterbodies and solving the problem of flood and drought in the nation?
- Would you like to be remembered for ensuring that our country is self-sufficient as far as energy consumption is concerned?

- Would you like to be remembered for creating a unique venture which can result in hundreds of enterprises?
- Would you like to be remembered for leading a movement of a 100 million youths for nation-building?
- Or will the future generations remember you for having revitalized the public healthcare system?

Later in 2009, when I started working with him, I began to realize that this was a common thread in the many speeches he delivered in schools and colleges. He would end by saying, 'Tonight, before you go to sleep, take a piece of paper or your laptop. Write down the answer to this question and mail it to me. If your answer is good, I will send you an autograph and a photograph!'

Most of the students he met had been posed this question at least once. But since I *worked* with him, I used to receive this question every now and then, sometimes once every week. And each time, after hearing my answer, he would say, 'Oh, you fellow! Build on it further. Enrich it from the last time. Add more value.'

This went on and on for a good six months, till I reached a point where my 'answer enrichment centre' was exhausted. I was simply out of ideas.

One day, on our way to an event in Kerala, Dr Kalam asked me his trademark question yet again. This time I decided to throw the ball back in his court. It was part defence and part exhaustion. 'I have answered this question so many times. Why don't you answer this question for a change? What would you like to be remembered for?' I couldn't help but smile at my cheeky response.

There was a short, unusual silence.

So I continued, 'Let me make it easier for you. Would you like to be remembered as a missile man, a nuclear man, a rocket engineer, a Bharat Ratna recipient, a President or an author?'

I thought I had covered all his achievements, but I still had a lot to learn about him. And that day I got a peek into his innermost thoughts, into the recesses of his mind.

'All your options are wrong,' he declared, taking me by surprise. I started recollecting all the facts I knew about him but I could not understand which aspect of his life I had missed. He cleared my confusion in the next sentence.

'The right option is not there in your list. I do not want to be remembered for any of these things.' And then, in an excited tone, he disclosed, 'I want to be remembered as a teacher. That is my goal.'

It occurred to me then that I had indeed missed the most obvious fact. Back in 2008, Dr Kalam was first introduced to me as my teacher, and it was the most significant role he played in my life, as he did in the lives of many others.

I did not stop my questions there.

I had one last question to ask him, to help me answer his pet question. 'How do I truly find what *I* will be remembered for?' I asked.

He then smiled and replied, 'That is difficult to say because the true answer will keep evolving. But I will tell you this. Get a diary or a notebook. Give it a name—something which is close to your heart, something which will remind you of what you want to become. Make it a habit to write down everything you learn, everything that inspires you, even things that trouble you, and everything you do to reach your long-term goals. Record all the small steps you take in your long and difficult journey. Especially keep a record of the times when you fail, so you remember your stumbling blocks. Note down the names of those people who pick you up when you fall—remember to be grateful always. In the years to come, you will look back at it all and smile. You might also be able to inspire others.'

The first thing that I did after that conversation was to buy a large notebook. I wrote about my dreams and aspirations. I named it after someone who will always be very close to my heart. I called it my Kalam Diary.

6

Critical Stakes Awaken Your Hidden Potential

During my tenure with Dr Kalam, I was mainly required to work on the speeches and lectures he delivered. I would collect and collate the relevant data for his lectures, structure and edit the entire document and then add final touches to it.

In February 2011, Dr Kalam had accepted an invitation to inaugurate the 30th Annual Conference of the Indian Society of Nephrology (ISN) in Puducherry. The function was scheduled to be held on 12 February, and Dr Kalam's flight to Chennai was scheduled for the 11th, since Chennai is the nearest airport to Puducherry.

On 9th morning, Dr Kalam came to the office and gave me a mountain of material on nephrology—the study of kidneys. He then said, 'Look, day after tomorrow, I am going to a conference organized by ISN. I want this to be a unique lecture that'll have fresh thoughts and the latest ideas. Can you give me a draft by tonight? Then we will discuss it tomorrow.'

Let me confess something here.

I know absolutely nothing about nephrology. It is Greek to me. I knew, however, that if I read up on the subject, I would get some understanding of it. But within a day? It seemed like an impossible task. I didn't have much of a choice, though, since he had to deliver his lecture in the next three days.

I was worrying about all this when he interrupted my thoughts. 'Good. I will look forward to the draft then.'

Before I could gather my thoughts, he left the room.

By 10.30 a.m. that day, I was immersed in Internet research. I was reading article after article on the subject, struggling through all the medical jargon and trying to make sense of it all. It was an uphill task, a race against time. I was at it till evening, sifting through innumerable articles and news items, jotting down points and taking notes. There was no time to eat, so I made do with a hasty snack of biscuits and coffee. By 10.30 p.m., I was thoroughly exhausted and incredibly hungry. In my view, I had become the quickest self-taught expert on nephrology!

I got an eight-page-long draft ready, took a print out, arranged the papers in order and went to the reading room, where I was sure I'd find Dr Kalam. And there he was, behind the usual pile of books, reading one of his favourite books—*Everyday Greatness* by Stephen Covey.

I wanted to have a quick discussion with him about the draft and then call it a day. I thought that if he was satisfied with the draft, then both of us would be relaxed the next day. I handed him the document and took the chair across from him, hoping he would like what he read. As I waited, my eyes strayed to the stack of books on his table, and I idly wondered at the effort it would take to pull the book at the very bottom without making the rest topple over.

'I've finished the draft,' he said, interrupting my thoughts, which felt scattered and all over the place after twelve hours of continuous work.

'And?' I asked.

'Well, you see, it is good for a first attempt. But now you should try to make it more interesting and insightful. It should capture the attention of the audience. I'll share my notes too, and then you can work on your next draft. We will discuss it in detail tomorrow.'

I was dejected. I had spent the whole day preparing the draft, but it had not met his expectations.

I went home and started working on it all over again. I didn't stop till 6.30 a.m. Once I was done, I emailed the reworked draft to him, slept for a few hours and was back in the office by 9 a.m.

Dr Kalam came to the office early that day, carrying the new draft with him.

Before I could ask him anything, he said, 'You, fellow, sent this at 6.35 a.m.! When did you sleep?'

I didn't reply.

He continued, 'I think I have put you through a lot of stress. I'm glad you worked on it; it is good now. It looks interesting. I knew this was a difficult topic.'

'It was indeed alien to me,' I agreed, feeling almost sorry for myself.

'Yes, but you know, sometimes, the most difficult of situations can bring out the best in us. It enables us to push ourselves beyond the familiar boundaries and discover hidden potential. I had a similar experience when I was working with my teacher long, long ago, when I was about your age.

'From 1954–57, I was studying aeronautical engineering at the Madras Institute of Technology (MIT), Chennai. In my third year, I, along with five other students, was assigned a project to design an attack aircraft which would fly at low levels. I was responsible for the aerodynamic and structural design of the project and the integration. The other five members of my team were designing the propulsion, control, guidance, avionics and instrumentation of the aircraft.'

He leaned back in his chair and continued to recount his story.

'The design teacher, Professor Srinivasan, the then director of MIT, was our guide. He reviewed the project and declared my work gloomy and disappointing. He wasn't ready to listen to the difficulties that I'd faced while collecting data from multiple designers. I asked for a month's time to complete the task, since I also had to get inputs from my teammates, without which I could not complete the system design. Professor Srinivasan told me, "Look, young man, today is Friday afternoon. I will give you three more days. If by Monday morning I don't get the configuration design, your scholarship will be stopped."

'I received a huge jolt. The scholarship was my lifeline; without it I wouldn't have been able to continue my studies. There was no other option for me but to finish the task within the appointed time. My team was forced to work round the clock. We didn't eat or sleep that night, and kept working on the drawing board throughout. On Saturday, I took just an hour's break. On Sunday morning, I was nearly done, when I felt someone's presence in my laboratory. It was Professor Srinivasan. He had come to assess my progress. After looking at my work, he patted my back and hugged me affectionately. And his praise made it all worth it. "I knew I was putting you under stress and asking you to meet a difficult deadline. But you have done a great job with the system design."

'Not only did Professor Srinivasan teach me about the necessity of valuing time, he also brought out the best in us. I realized that when something critical is at stake, the human mind gets ignited and its capacity increases manifold. That's exactly what happened with me. It is one of the techniques of discovering and honing talent.'

He concluded, 'And this is what has happened with you today. Today, you have not only learnt about a new science, but more importantly, you have pushed yourself outside your comfort zone and discovered that you're capable of a lot more than you thought. You have done well. Now let's work on this lecture and perfect it.'

That day we rang all the nephrologists we knew. We spoke with the specialists and put together a masterpiece. Two days later, a rocket engineer and missile scientist spoke confidently to an assembly of senior nephrologists about the best technologies in kidney care. And the audience was left spellbound.

At the end, he delivered an oath to the spirited audience, whose average age was above fifty:

'. . . I will be a lifelong learner, I will practise what I learn and I will train my team to be competent . . . and I will not introduce any diagnostic pain.'

As the audience applauded, I made a new entry in my Kalam Diary—critical stakes ignite the mind and awaken hidden potential. Difficulty cannot be handled by being scared of how high the peak is. It can be tackled by drawing a path to the peak, and when you toil in the process of scaling that height, you learn and grow.

7

The Old General with
Bright Ideas

One of Dr Kalam's closest friends since his DRDO days[1] was Major General R. Swaminathan. They had known each other since 1982. He lived at Dr Kalam's residence, just across the back garden and remained Dr Kalam's trusted adviser all the way to the Rashtrapati Bhavan, and even after that.

I had first met him in 2008, during our first class at IIMA. He was nicknamed the Old General, the one with the 'most youthful and firebrand ideas'.

A tall, lanky man with bushy, white eyebrows, Major General Swaminathan was a man with an exceptional memory. We were all amazed to know that he could remember the exact dates on which Dr Kalam had delivered his speeches—even the ones that were delivered several years ago. Not only that, he remembered the content of the speeches as well, with absolute accuracy! He was extremely

---

[1] Defence Research and Development Organisation

knowledgeable and was well versed in a wide range of subjects: religion, technology, defence and travel. He was a very animated and enthusiastic speaker.

Due to a medical mishap during a small surgery, Major General Swaminathan had lost complete mobility and strength in one of his legs. He had difficulty walking and needed support to move around. His office was located on the first floor, and he often struggled while taking the stairs. But in spite of his difficulties, he didn't want to shift his office to the ground floor, nor did he ever use a wheelchair.

From 2009 to the beginning of 2011, I worked with Major General R. Swaminathan, doing joint research for innumerable speeches and our many books. He played an instrumental role in drafting many of Dr Kalam's best speeches.

Major General Swaminathan would sit on a brown swivel chair behind a desk near the door. Dr Kalam would sit across the same desk on a lounge chair. I would mostly be at the other end of this small office set-up, away from the entrance. This was how we would seat ourselves and have long discussions while preparing every speech. When Dr Kalam was not around, Major General Swaminathan and I would casually chat about this and that.

It was during these chats I came to realize that he was very well versed in Hindu theology. He once told me that there are six vices in Hindu theology, called *Arishadvarga*, which prevent man from attaining moksha (salvation). He counted them on his fingers: kama (lust), *krodha* (anger), *lobh* (greed), *moha* (attachment), *mada* or *ahankar* (pride) and *maatsarya* (jealousy). This knowledge will stay with me forever.

Our work was often interspersed with light moments. There is one such hilarious incident that comes to mind. In early 2011, Dr Kalam and I were in Indore for a series of lectures at IIM. One of these lectures was about to begin at 2 p.m. At about 1.30 p.m., just after lunch, we realized that there was a particular presentation that should have been added in the lecture. However, when we searched on our laptops, that presentation was missing. Somehow, it hadn't been transferred along with the rest of the documents in that folder.

In our Delhi office, there was a backup that had all the files, lectures and presentations from years ago. We immediately called up the Delhi office to request them to send us the file via email. However, Major General Swaminathan was not available on the phone. He was not responding to our emails either. We were running out of time and had barely ten minutes to the lecture.

So I decided to access his computer remotely.

Some time back, I had created a digital bridge for remote-access login to the server. I took out my mobile phone and downloaded some applications and toolkit. This was a simple TeamViewer connection that required the use of just a mobile phone. But back then this technology was considered almost a marvel.

Soon, the computer in Delhi started to simulate the operations of my mobile. Major General Swaminathan would probably have returned to his computer by then and found that he had lost control of his computer—the cursor was moving without his command and the files were opening in front of his bewildered eyes without his instructions! In fact, some files were getting sent to me via email without his intervention. He must have been shocked and thoroughly confused, which is probably why Dr Kalam received an urgent call from him, saying, 'The computers are out of control.'

Dr Kalam asked him to calm down and told him that it was just us. He could not believe it, and later, when I was back in Delhi, he made me perform the 'trick' again. Only then did he believe me!

Later that month, Major General Swaminathan lost his wife to a stroke. It made me acutely aware of how fragile our lives are. And it was very disquieting to realize that these wise men, who had become so much a part of my life and whose company I took for granted, wouldn't always be around. It made me uneasy.

The grief of losing the person he was closest to took a toll on The Old General's health. A week later, he developed complications and had to be taken to hospital. Dr Kalam personally oversaw the treatment of his friend. When things did not improve, he was sent to the CARE hospital in Hyderabad, which had been started by some old colleagues of Dr Kalam's.

The General remained at CARE for almost the whole of 2011.

Dr Kalam would say to us, 'He has a sharp mind, but loneliness is a powerful weapon of mental deterioration. You fellows should keep him busy.' And so Dr Kalam and his team would call him regularly and ask for advice on various matters. This soon grew into a ritual that we performed daily, before starting work. Major General Swaminathan was happy, on his part, to still be on 'active duty'.

As 2012 dawned, we started wondering whether the seventy-three-year-old general would ever recover fully. The general went through one complication after another. But he battled on like the soldier he was. And soon, there was some positive news from his doctors. That put a smile on all our faces.

By mid-2012, after spending almost sixteen months in Hyderabad, the General returned to Delhi. A celebration was held in his honour when he returned to the office.

Things went reasonably well for the next three months. Then, in November 2012, a month after Dr Kalam's birthday, Major General Swaminathan took ill once again. He lost mobility in his other leg too, and was bedridden. He was immediately sent to the military hospital in Delhi but his recovery was slow.

Everyone in the office was extremely worried. We visited him regularly at the hospital and tried to cheer him up. We felt helpless, though—we desperately wanted to help, to see him happy, but there was very little we could actually do to make it better for him.

One day, when I came back to the office after paying a visit to the hospital, Dr Kalam asked me, 'How is he?'

I told him the truth. 'He is trying, but nothing seems to be happening.' I was visibly dejected.

'He is a fighter. We are all children of God. Remember, when God is with you, no one can stand against you,' he replied.

Major General Swaminathan struggled for the next four months. In the second week of February, he lost consciousness, owing to multiple organ failure, and the chances of his survival were bleak. The doctors told us to get in touch with his two sons, who were abroad, and ask them to come back immediately.

One son made it in time and could meet his father before he passed away. But the other one was a few hours late, and when I saw his inconsolable sorrow, I realized the importance of bidding a final goodbye to our loved ones. Major General Swaminathan passed away on 15 February 2013.

It was a sad day for all of us. Dr Kalam ensured that all arrangements were made for his last rites. Later that day he put out a message along with a photograph in the old General's memory on his website and social media pages.

'It is a sad day for me. I have lost a very good friend of mine. May his soul rest in peace.'

Major General Swaminathan's sons took care of all his belongings, and soon his house on the other side of the garden was vacated. His brown swivel chair was left untouched, as a tribute to his memory. No one used his chair or his desk again. Dr Kalam insisted that these relics not be removed. 'He was brave to the core and never let his pain come in the way of his untiring work,' he would often say about his friend.

Most of the people in our office thought that Dr Kalam would get the chair and table removed in a few days, once he got over the grief of losing his friend. But two and half years after his death, till 27 July 2015—the day Dr Kalam himself passed away—the General's chair still remained where he had left it.

Dr Kalam had missed the occupant of that chair till the very end. Even death and time could not weaken the bond he had shared with his friend.

On 28 July, the morning after Dr Kalam's death, when I arrived at his house, I saw that the general's chair had finally been moved to another room.

The Old General's duty had finally come to an end.

8

Think Solution—Even if It Is Compact

I always accompanied Dr Kalam on his teaching programmes. On many occasions, we even delivered the lectures together. He would speak for about forty to forty-five minutes and then ask me to speak to the class for the next ten minutes. I always found it a challenge to hold the students' attention with him sitting behind me. But the moment he sensed the class losing interest, he would become a student himself and ask me a question on the subject that I was discussing. It was his way of getting the students to focus on the speaker.

Often we would design his courses in such a way that they included three to four lectures and some student presentations as well. The one thing he always insisted on was that the subject in discussion be relevant, contemporary and interesting. This meant extensive research on current affairs and a careful analysis of the trending debates and opinions. It took multiple iterations on our part for the lessons to finally take shape. In many cases we had to create more than twenty lesson plans before we were satisfied with the course we'd arrived at. And then too, it would be 'enriched' minutes before the class. Such last-minute improvements would occur mostly in the car, on our way to the class. A lot of times he would look at the questions framed for his students and say, 'We have not designed them properly. Make them interesting. Designing the problem is the most important step, which needs 80 per cent of our attention.' After a small pause, he'd continue, 'If we don't contemplate enough to frame the right questions, the students will not apply themselves enough to come up with well-thought-out answers.'

We had one of our best classes in April 2010, at the Gatton College of Business and Economics, University of Kentucky, USA. It was especially interesting for me because it was my first trip abroad as part of Team Kalam. It was the longest journey that we had ever taken together—it lasted for seventeen days.

Gatton College is located in the small city of Lexington, in the state of Kentucky, well known for the brand Kentucky Fried Chicken (KFC). Kentucky also enjoys a global reputation for its horses, racehorses in particular. The dark-coloured grass of Kentucky often looks blue in the fading sunlight, and that is why it is also called the Bluegrass State.

The course titled Evolution of a Peaceful and Prosperous World comprised a couple of lectures by him, and there were many long and high-quality presentations by the students as well, on various topics of international significance. These presentations were to be made in two rounds—one at the start of the course, when we would give them our feedback. And then once more, at the end of the course, after incorporating our feedback and listening to the lectures.

The student presentation that had fascinated Dr Kalam the most was about harnessing energy from chicken waste. The report was presented by two students. And we were amazed to see the minute detailing that had gone into their presentation. After discussing different technologies that could work in a rural setting, they concluded, '. . . each chicken creates enough daily waste to power one electric bulb for twenty minutes every day. Thus the business will break even in less than one year.'

Dr Kalam and I were both astounded by the finding. Their enterprise-oriented approach and focus on looking for solutions were commendable. Dr Kalam wholeheartedly praised the students and felt very content and proud to be a teacher.

That presentation remained in his memory for a very long time. About four months later, in September 2010, we went to IIM, Ahmedabad, for the third edition of the GRIIT course. It was extra special for me because I had done the same course two years back. This time he delivered three lectures, and there were seventeen student presentations. Both of us listened to the presentations, questioned the students and made suggestions.

That night when we were at the dinner table, I noticed that Dr Kalam was not his usual excited self, even though he'd spent the whole day with his students. At around 11 p.m. we stepped out for a post-dinner walk in the small garden. I could not resist and asked him, 'Sir, you don't seem to have liked the presentations.' He did not stop walking, and replied without a break in his stride, 'No. Not that. They were great. All the presentations show great research and good thinking. But I am concerned. Almost all the presentations aim at a very large target, which is good. However, when it comes to solutions, they simply talk about the need to change the policies, the business environment or the law itself. All the solutions took changes at the macro level as a given, thus making for incomplete solutions.'

He stopped walking, turned around and started moving back to the guest house. 'Young minds should not become so dependent on the environment such that it shapes and restricts their solutions. Instead, they should shape the environment with their minds. Remember Gatton College's chicken-waste solution? I liked it because it was a solution in totality—it was an enterprise-oriented approach which needed no environment shifts. Young minds should be bold enough to face the situation as it is and strong enough to shape their situations themselves. Think of solutions which you can implement alone and avoid making grand plans which require the globe to tilt for you. Pocket-sized solutions which walk are better than wardrobe-sized plans that squat.'

This was another lesson that found its place in my Kalam Diary. Dr Kalam wanted the Indian youth to become more enterprising and proactive and look for solutions themselves, without waiting for the situation to miraculously become favourable. The solutions may be small in scale to begin with, but as long as they work, it doesn't matter. Grand journeys always begin with one small step. He wanted the youth to be capable, humble and courageous; he wanted them to be strong enough to take the first step, without being afraid of the environment collapsing around them.

9

Greatest Bliss

I have many cherished memories from our Kentucky trip in 2010.

The structure of the course was such that each student group was required to select one topic from the list we gave them and then make a half-an-hour-long presentation on the subject chosen. They would discuss the presentation with Dr Kalam and me in a small meeting room. Along with them would be Professor Walter J. Ferrier, popularly called Wally, the course coordinator.

One of the students in that programme was a young girl, not very tall, with golden hair. Her name was Stephanie and she always had a smile on her face. Before she moved to Gatton College to study, she had been a member of the District Education Board and had a career in teaching. She was one of the most active members of the class. Her presentation was on how to improve the public-school system in the United States.

She had done significant research on the US education system and discovered some alarming gaps, even though their system is relatively well-developed. Being a teacher herself, she had many ideas on how to improve the performance in primary schools. Her research showed that even though America was home to almost half the Nobel laureates, it was lagging behind other countries in educating the next generation of learners. This was evident from the fact that American schools ranked twenty-ninth in the global science score, among fifty-seven participating schools from different countries.

During our meeting, she told us that she wanted to go back to the education sector after her graduation, and Dr Kalam appreciated her decision. He said, 'It is good to see that you want to use your education to improve education!'

Her presentation was extremely powerful and left everyone impressed. After the discussion, Dr Kalam asked her, 'Do you have any questions?' There was a slight pause. Then she reached inside her bag and pulled out a copy of Dr Kalam's autobiography, *Wings of Fire*. She said, 'I have read this from cover to cover. I see that you have many achievements. It is indeed remarkable. You have pioneered many projects. But I want to ask you a personal question. Which one of these achievements would you say is closest to your heart and gave you the greatest joy?'

It was a very interesting question, and everyone in the room silently waited for his answer. He finally replied, 'Great question, Stephanie. This is one of the best questions a student has ever asked me. You see, I have worked on many projects, and to answer your question I will have to take you through some points in my life.

'Two decades ago, while I was working at the Indian Space Research Organization (ISRO), I got the kind of education that can't be received at any university. I will narrate an incident to you. I was given a task by Professor Satish Dhawan—to develop the first satellite launch vehicle, SLV-3, which could put the Satellite Rohini in orbit.

'It was one of the largest high-technology space programmes undertaken in 1973. The whole community of space technologists geared up for this task. Thousands of scientists, engineers and technicians were working together, which resulted in the actualization of the first SLV-3 launch on 10 August 1979. SLV-3 took off in the early hours and the first stage worked out beautifully. But the mission could not achieve its objective, as the control system malfunctioned in the second stage.

'There was a press conference held at Sriharikota after that event. Professor Dhawan took me to that press conference. And there, in front of the media, he took the entire blame for the failure of that mission, even though it was I who should have been held responsible because I was the project-and-mission director.

'On 18 July 1980, when we managed to launch the SLV-3, successfully launching the Rohini into orbit, there was another press conference, and that time Professor Dhawan pushed me into the limelight. What we learn from this is that a leader gives the credit for success to those who work for it, while he takes the blame on himself for their failures. That is leadership. The scientific community in India has had the fortune to work under such great leaders, which has resulted in many accomplishments for us. That success gave all of us a lot of joy.

'The second instance that made me happy is about a missile system. On 11 April 1999, the Agni-II took off under the command of computers. Six hundred parameters from the missile were being monitored in real time, through a series of radars, telemetry stations and ship-borne instruments, all of which were networked with our own communication satellites. The Agni, along with its payload, managed to reach the pre-determined target 2000 kilometres away. An important success like that was brought about by the partnership between various labs in academic institutions and industries across India. That was a triumph of our self-reliance at a time when we were being denied technological help by several developed countries.

'In May 1998, the then chairman of Atomic Energy Commission (AEC), Dr R. Chidambaram, and I were working on the results of some underground nuclear tests. We were very close to the test site and the countdown was running. At T-5 seconds, hundreds of parameters from different instrumentations were being displayed on the computer monitors. The project was about to take off in a few seconds. At T-0, we witnessed the whole earth shake and thunder around us. It felt like a part of the earth was rising.

What powerful energy India had generated through nuclear weapons! That was another achievement that made me and my team very happy.

'Through the 1990s, I was the chairman of the Technology Information Forecasting and Assessment Council (TIFAC). The council evolved with the help of experts. A road map was prepared on how to transform India into a developed country by 2020. Nearly twenty volumes worth of documents were generated and presented to the then Prime Minister in 1996. There were some experimental projects mentioned in those documents, for which funds had been allocated. Those funds were utilized to multiply the sugar-cane quality and production per hectare in Bihar and the milk production in Punjab. All those projects which were a part of India's Millennium Mission 2020 had generated a keen interest in the country. On 15 August 2003, our Prime Minister announced that India would become a developed nation by 2020. This also gave me tremendous happiness.

'But the most important event that I would like to share with you is the development of the Floor Reaction Orthosis (FRO) caliper—artificial limbs—for children with polio. During my visit to one of the hospitals in Hyderabad, I found out that many children were struggling to walk with artificial limbs that weighed over 3 kilogram. At the request of Professor Prasad, the head of the orthopaedic department at Nizam's Institute of Medical Science, I discussed with my Agni friends whether the composite material that was used for making the heat shield of Agni could be used for fabricating FROs for polio patients. They immediately said that it was possible.

'We worked on that project for some time and came up with an FRO for children, which weighed around 300 grams. The doctors fitted the new lightweight FRO on a little girl and she started walking and running around freely again. Her parents were present there too. Tears of joy rolled down their faces when they saw their daughter run around with the light caliper. With the lightweight device provided by the hospital, she could run, ride a bicycle and do all the things she had been unable to do for so long. Reducing that child's pain and watching her be free meant more to me than all the other events that I told you about just now.'

Stephanie smiled. We all did. It was indeed a gratifying answer.

I realized something that day: a great scientist is one who is also sensitive.

Later that evening, this incident made its way into my Kalam Diary. Dr Kalam had achieved greatness not just because of his intelligence. Anyone can be intelligent. He was great because of his high emotional involvement. Great achievers are not merely smart or productive; they are unimaginably sensitive and compassionate. Emotions directed towards a specific goal make such people more determined; it enables them to push themselves and deliver results far beyond their wildest imagination.

10

April Bloomers

This is another story about our trip to Kentucky. Our team comprised Dr Kalam, Dhanshyam, his personal assistant and I. Dhanshyam had been associated with Dr Kalam since his Rashtrapati Bhavan days. He was a poet at heart, and could sing and mimic people extremely well. Besides managing schedules efficiently, he had the capacity to make anyone smile. In another life, perhaps he could have had a great career in Bollywood!

In terms of area, Kentucky is the thirty-seventh largest state of America, out of all the fifty states. Interestingly, the state is famous for its horses, most of which are used for professional races all over the world. Kentucky horses are considered amongst the most expensive ones in the world and, during our stay, we read about a horse that was being sold for over $4 million—almost the value of ten Rolls-Royces!

April is a beautiful time in Kentucky, and we were lucky to have visited the state in that month.

Everywhere we looked, there were trees exploding with colourful flowers. The grass was lush; the surface of still ponds was covered with fallen leaves, through which ducks were gracefully treading their way with a trail of ducklings following behind them in a disciplined line. Stallions were grazing on the expansive meadows, occasionally looking up to watch the cars whiz past. The landscape brought sheer joy to our hearts.

In the middle of our tour, we visited the University of Louisville, where Dr Kalam was conferred with an honorary doctorate degree. The ceremony was followed by another lecture. Louisville, the largest city in the state, is about 120 kilometres from Lexington. Broad highways, known as superhighways, connect the two cities. They were lined with hundreds of small trees on either side, which were so full of flowers that one couldn't even see the leaves. As an admirer of flora, Dr Kalam was immediately attracted to the foliage. We were travelling with our hosts, Dr Viji and Dr Suvas Desai. Dr Kalam pointed at one of the trees and asked them, 'This is such a beautiful tree. What is it called? It is overflowing with blossoms.'

One of our hosts replied, 'Sir, this is called dogwood.'

Dr Kalam was not too pleased with this name. So he tried again, 'And that fellow with the pink flowers?'

This time, the other host interjected, 'That is also dogwood. In fact, all these trees are dogwoods, sir. Dogwood is the state flower and it is unique to Kentucky.'

'Then why would you call it dogwood? I don't think the trees like that name,' Dr Kalam said. 'You should petition your Governor to call it something else. I am sure that I will meet him again soon—should I speak to him?'

Everybody nodded in agreement.

Later that evening, after dinner, Dr Kalam surprisingly brought up the subject of the trees again. 'It is *such* a beautiful tree—why is it called dogwood?' Then he looked at me and said, 'Funny guy, get your computer. Ask Google.'

'Asking Google' was something we did very often, along with 'asking Wikipedia'. Whenever there was any confusion over a topic, Dr Kalam would promptly say, 'Google will tell you. Let us ask him.'

So I fired up my laptop and we soon found out how such a vibrant tree had got its relatively dull name. The tree, having slender branches, was earlier used to make dags—daggers— and hence it was originally named Dagwood, which over time got distorted to 'dogwood'.

'That's unfortunate. Imagine if someone did this to our names. The whole meaning of our names would change. My own name will start sounding like that of a pen!'[1] He exclaimed at our new-found information. 'In the last fifteen days, these trees have given us so much joy and happiness. Now let us try to give something back to our new friends. Why don't we write a poem and give them a new name?'

---

[1] 'Kalam' means 'pen' in Hindi.

It was touching to see his sensitivity towards a flower-bearing tree in a distant land, which, in all likelihood we wouldn't even visit again. And thus, to write a poem for the dogwood, we listed many names that we thought the tree would like. After coming up with some dozen names, Dr Kalam finally hit the jackpot—he called it the April Bloomer! Once the name was decided, the poem flowed through his pen effortlessly. The poem was titled 'Blossomed to Give'.

Blossomed to Give

O my young friends, white and pink flowers,
I witness your beauty everywhere.
Cheering the hearts and,
Bringing smiles to faces.
O my young friend, 'What is your name?' I asked.
'O Kalam, dear Kalam, in bluegrass
They call us dogwood;
But as the children of spring,
We are the April Bloomers.'

—A.P.J. Abdul Kalam

During the rest of our stay in Kentucky, Dr Kalam never called the April Bloomer by its original name. He even encouraged others to call it by its new name. He told the mayor, the professors and even the Governor of the state that they should consider renaming the dogwood the April Bloomer.

When we were leaving, Dr Kalam looked out at the trees through the car window and said, 'I think the flowers are happier with their new name. Don't you think so? They will remember us. We have done a good job.'

Just then, I pulled out a surprise for him that the hotel staff had helped me put together—a small bouquet of April Bloomers in assorted colours. I said, 'Here is their gratitude.'

He smiled. We never met the April Bloomers again.

Years later, I ran into one of our hosts in Delhi and he said to me, 'Many people in Kentucky now call the dogwood April Bloomer. It seems like your mission has been successful.'

11

Water Is a Life-Giver

During our Kentucky stay, the organizers had reserved one afternoon for a trip to Lake Cumberland. They were very excited to show us the lake, April being the best month to visit it. Our hosts had arranged a small cruiser for us as their families were also coming along.

Dr Kalam was always apprehensive about leisure trips. Whenever we were abroad and a visit to a place of interest was suggested, he would predictably refuse, saying, 'I am here to work' or 'Don't make the host spend on these things.' When I would turn to him—disappointment across my face—he would add hastily, probably feeling bad, 'But you fellows can go. I will give you leave. Go wherever you want. Tell me what you see.'

It was indeed difficult to convince him to come along with us, and called for some trickery. One good way to tempt him into such leisure trips was to say that the outing would help him write his next few speeches or help him work on his next lessons. This approach worked most of the time but I was unsure about it at that moment.

So when the organizers told me excitedly that they wanted to finalize the time and date of the cruise trip to Lake Cumberland, I knew immediately that Dr Kalam would turn it down. Needing to present the leisure trip as a 'knowledge gain' trip, I began my research. The Internet told me that the lake covered an area of over 265 square kilometres, had a shoreline of over 2000 kilometres, and had enough water to cover the entire state of Kentucky up to a height of 3 inches. I also found out that Lake Cumberland was a part of a large network of rivers and lakes, which was fed by a water management system operated by the US government. It was actually a man-made reservoir used for tourism, flood control and power generation. I had hit the bull's eye! This was all the information I needed to lure Dr Kalam.

At dinner that night, I circuitously broached the subject. 'Sir, there is this amazing lake here, which is fed by a water management system. It is a functional example of the sort of interconnected water management system that you have been proposing for Bihar!'

'Where is it?' he asked. I smiled to myself. I had triggered his curiosity.

'Not far. It's about an hour or so away from here—called Lake Cumberland.'

I had hoped that he would enquire more but I was met with silence. I wasn't ready to accept defeat, so I pushed on.

'In fact, Dr Viji, Dr Desai and their families are going to see it tomorrow. We will be free at that time. I think we should go too. It will be a good topic to discuss with the students whom you will be addressing a couple of days later.'

'If it is on our way to Louisville, we can drive by,' he said without enthusiasm.

I was almost there! Now I just had to get him on the boat.

'I think we should spend more time there and observe the lake in its entirety. Maybe we should see where they feed the water into the lake—that is important. They are taking a boat to the lake; we should hop on for a while. Right?' I asked, hoping to seal the deal.

'But *where* does the water come from? Is there a river?' he asked.

I was stumped. I had not done research on the source of water for the mighty lake. Whatever little I knew, I told him. 'I think it comes from a river management system, somewhere in the west. I will find out more.'

'Okay,' he said and I immediately called up our host to inform him that we were going ahead with the trip.

The next morning we drove to the lake, where a small cruiser was waiting for us. The families of both our hosts were already there. As we were boarding, Dr Kalam quipped, 'This is a big boat.'

We spent a lovely, sunny hour on the cruiser. On the lower deck, the captain of the ship invited us to the control room. Being a curious soul, Dr Kalam accepted the offer.

After quizzing the captain about his boat, he took control of the wheel himself. Once he was satisfied with the experience, I said to him, 'Sir, you will make a good captain!' He smiled at my compliment.

Then he requested our captain to show him how the water was fed into the lake. The captain explained that a complex system of locks and dams existed along the river. This system was used to control the water flow and save the state from floods.

'We must study this procedure for the state of Bihar,' he said, after listening to the captain. The state of Bihar was very close to his heart. His primary focus was on solving the problem of floods and droughts which plagued the state on a regular basis. His solution to Bihar's flooding problem was a 'better water management system, covering the lakes and rivers in the state'. Time and again, he had presented his plans to the state MPs and MLAs, but little was done to actualize any. He saw hope in the water management system of Kentucky—he thought that an actual working model would kindle a stronger desire among the Bihar authorities for the implementation of his plans.

Sensing Dr Kalam's curiosity, our hosts asked me if he would be interested to see the lock-and-dam system that the captain had earlier talked about. This time I was in no doubt. 'Of course!' I replied.

A week later, on our way to Louisville, we made a stopover at a US Army Base, called the McAlpine Lock and Dam. There we were shown the system of water locks that we had briefly learnt about earlier. A senior US Army officer elaborated on the design and purpose of the water locks.

Rivers are irregular in gradient, shallow at some points and deeper at others. This makes it impossible for larger ships to move along these rivers smoothly. So, under the river management system, the riverbed is evened, the silt is dredged out and the waterbodies are connected. Finally, different sections of the river—which are at different heights—are connected through locks.

A ship approaching from a higher level is 'locked' in a watertight compartment. Then the water in the lock is gradually released to make the water level go down till it matches the level of the river downstream. It is like an elevator for large ships.

The McAlpine Lock and Dam and its canal system was the first major engineering project on the Ohio River, and was completed in 1830. It was designed in such a way that the shipping traffic could navigate the rivers easily, moving from one city to another along the waterbody. The locks were expanded, first by a private company and then by the US Army Corps of Engineers. The system (previously called the Louisville and Portland Canal) was renamed as the McAlpine Lock and Dam in 1960, in honour of William McAlpine, who was the only civilian to have ever served as District Engineer of the Corps of Louisville.

We were highly impressed to know that this complicated and ingenious system was almost two centuries old! It was because of this system that Louisville and its surrounding areas had been safe from regular flooding for the past fifty years. The officer showed us a board which declared that the 'transportation cost via land is one-tenth that of air. And the transportation cost via waterway is one-tenth that of land'. This information became a major motivation for Dr Kalam to propose a similar system in India, which would make transportation between cities economical.

As we were about to leave, the officer who was showing us the system said something that made a lasting impression on us. 'I read Adam Smith, the famous economist,' he said. 'He says that it was some province in eastern India which was the pioneer in river navigation.' The eastern region that he was referring to was the state of Bengal, and Adam Smith had indeed mentioned it in his work. Five years later, that inspiring fact became an important anchor for our book, *Advantage India*.

Later that month, when we returned to Delhi, Dr Kalam spent many hours explaining the McAlpine Lock and Dam system to several leaders. He wrote letters about it to dignitaries, including the Prime Minister. He strongly believed that he had seen a water management system which could be implemented in India, especially in Bihar.

That experience remained etched in his memory till the very end, and he spoke about it at numerous gatherings. The inability of the governments in power to understand the long-term merit of a major water management system despite success stories from around the world caused Dr Kalam great disappointment. Yet, he still pursued the grand idea of a comprehensive system for India's waterways throughout his residency, and even beyond it. He used to say, 'Someday a young, thinking, visionary leader will come and do this project for the nation. We have the power to make water a life-giver and not a life-taker.'

Eighty per cent of India's rainfall happens within a span of about a hundred hours. We cannot choose what cards are dealt to us, but we can decide how to play them. Floods and droughts are frequent across India and, within the last decade, fatal floods have hit Tamil Nadu, Odisha, Uttarakhand, Jammu and Kashmir, the Northeast, Bihar, Maharashtra and Gujarat. Thousands have lost their lives, many have been rendered homeless and thousands of crores of property has been demolished. All of this could have been avoided with a better water management system. And this is what he believed would become an important issue to the India of 2020. Even today, with news of flood and drought affecting different parts of India every year, most agree that a better lake-and-river management system is a need—but none seem to have the comprehensive understanding and conviction to pursue such a project. Dr Kalam's words come to mind, 'We must manage our water better . . . Water should be a life-giver and not a life-taker.'

---

*

Bihar Farmers Study Trip

Dr Kalam held Bihar very close to his heart; he could envision many opportunities for the state and also feel the pain of its people. I visited many parts of Bihar with him from 2009 to 2015. I worked with him on several speeches and plans that we formulated for the state. I have witnessed the love and hope he had for Bihar, especially for the youth and the farmers. Even when he was not in Bihar, its welfare was always on his mind.

In 2010, Dr Kalam and I attended the inauguration of Warana PURA in Maharashtra, a unique place run by a cooperative society. They've achieved total literacy and eradication of poverty for all 1,50,000 citizens in the area! Dr Kalam was really impressed by this initiative. A few days before the event, we had a meeting with a few professors— from IIM Ahmedabad—about how farmers could be empowered through management and technology.

After returning from Warana, Dr Kalam told me, 'We should ensure that the farmers of Bihar are empowered by the best minds of the nation.' And so we planned a trip for a group of young farmers from Paliganj, Bihar, to IIM Ahmedabad, and then to Warana, near Kolhapur. This was sponsored by Dr Kalam himself. Once the group of Bihar farmers completed their educational trip, Dr Kalam even called them up and quizzed them on what they had learnt; I was the intermediary translator in this conversation. After getting satisfactory replies, he asked them what they wanted from the government now. The Bihar farmers responded, 'We don't want free stuff—no free power or fertilizers—we want better technology and better access to markets!'

Dr Kalam repeated this message to all the stakeholders of Bihar—the district collectors, the ministers and even the Chief Minister. He stood for the slogan that for a developed India, we need a developed and happy Bihar.

———————— ✳ ————————

12

There Is a Fellow in There!

Dr Kalam was particularly attentive to the state of Odisha. Perhaps this was so because he had experienced some of his finest moments in that state. Wheeler Island was approximately 150 kilometres from Bhubaneswar,[1] the capital of Odisha, and it was where he had earned the title 'Missile Man'. He had also led a programme for developing and deploying five missile projects on Wheeler Island, including the 1989 launch of Agni.

Dr Kalam participated in many programmes in Odisha. His love for the state kept calling him back to it. We had conducted programmes in pretty much every part of the state, even in districts like Kalahandi. There is one particular incident that had occurred during one of our visits there, the memory of which still makes me smile.

Dr Kalam had accepted an invitation from the National Institute of Technology (NIT), Rourkela, to inaugurate their Technology Incubation Centre. The event was scheduled

[1] The island was aptly renamed Abdul Kalam Island in late 2015.

for 16 January 2010. Rourkela, situated in northern Odisha, borders Jharkhand. We had planned to fly from Delhi to Bhubaneswar and then hop on to a chopper at about 3 p.m. to reach Rourkela before 4.30 p.m.

During our flight from Delhi to Bhubaneswar, we discussed everything about Rourkela. It's a city with a population of 5 lakh people, famous for manufacturing steel. Dr Kalam asked me, 'Do you know why it is called Rourkela?'

Now, all I knew about Rourkela was that it was a newly founded city and was known for its industrial strength—but I was clueless about the origin of its name. So I replied in the negative.

That's when he told me the story of the city.

The steel mills of Rourkela were built by the Germans and the design of these mills were similar to the ones found in the German industrial town of Ruhr. The second half of the city's name was inspired from the word 'kella', meaning 'fort'. So, essentially, the city was called 'Ruhrkella', which eventually became Rourkela. Much of our time in the Bhubaneswar-bound flight was spent discussing the history and future of the city. Upon landing, we received news that the weather conditions around the Rourkela helipad were not suitable for flying and so we had to wait. We went to the airport lounge and made ourselves comfortable. Half an hour later, the weather conditions were still grim.

By 4 p.m., we were warned that if the sky did not clear within the next fifteen minutes, we would have to cancel the helicopter trip as visibility would be too low by the time we would reach Rourkela. I said to Dr Kalam, 'Sir, it looks like we will have to cancel the trip today. There is no way we can reach the function tomorrow morning in time. Shall I ask them to delay it?'

As always, he replied with a smile and cracked a joke to ease the situation. 'You fellow, ask the clouds to go away!' Then he looked out of the large glass door at the entrance of the lounge and said, 'Don't worry, we have fifteen minutes more. We cannot disappoint the engineers—think about it. They are looking forward to our arrival. We shouldn't keep them waiting.'

But there was little that any of us could do in that situation. Another ten minutes passed, and we were beginning to lose hope.

Then Dr Kalam suddenly rose to his feet and said, 'We can take a train.'

It was a startling idea—it would be an overnight journey through a Naxal area. But it was our only chance of making it to the event on time. I found out that the next train leaving for Rourkela was the Tapaswini Express and it would get us there by early next morning. I had never been on a train journey with Dr Kalam before. We were both apprehensive, but excited, about it.

News of Dr Kalam's intended train journey spread rapidly, and soon the media got wind of it. When we got to the train station, a sea of people stood waiting to greet us—about six to eight thousand of them. All had heard about Dr Kalam's train travel in the local media and had turned up to see him. They thronged the entire railway station and it was with great difficulty that we managed to reach the stationmaster's office. We waited there while the luggage was taken in. Dr Kalam kept glancing at his watch. 'I hope we don't miss the train. Shall we move?' he asked.

In a matter of minutes, we were asked to board the train. The distance from the stationmaster's office to the train was hardly 50 metres, but it was quite a task to walk through the huge crowd. In trying to greet Dr Kalam, people were pushing and shoving us. He moved slowly, shaking as many hands as he could. Soon we were aboard the train.

It was a first-class AC coach, comfortable but old. Dr Kalam was assigned a personal cabin while the rest of the entourage from Delhi, including me, was in the adjoining cabin. After ensuring that everything was in order in his cabin, such as the bedding, I stood outside talking to the security personnel. Those gun-toting young men were slightly tense because we were about to journey through an area fraught with unrest. And their anxiety was further elevated by the fact that Dr Kalam's train journey had been publicized far and wide already.

Before I continue with the account of our travels aboard the Tapaswini Express, let me explain a particular quirk of Dr Kalam's. Dr Kalam, as we all know by now, had a unique habit of using the word 'fellow' to address someone. He referred to anyone and anything as 'fellow', especially if he didn't know them personally. For instance, whenever monkeys would invade our Rajaji Marg office in Delhi, he would warn us, 'Those fellows are there, don't go that way'. Those of us who worked with him knew how to pick up on his exclusive references. But not everyone understood his language. The incident aboard the Rourkela-bound train is related to this habit of his.

Around 11 p.m., while I was talking to the nervous security personnel, Dr Kalam suddenly rushed out of his cabin. He looked around, located me and said, 'There is a fellow in my coach.'

Before I could decipher who the 'fellow' could be, the guards had jumped to their feet. Three security guards, with their rifles at the ready, burst into Dr Kalam's cabin. A moment later they came out, puzzled. There was no one in the cabin! Since it was the President himself who had made the claim, they were still alert, clutching their guns tightly. They went back in for another round, and this time they looked under the sheets, blankets and seats, and even behind the door of that small cabin. As the search continued, I turned to Dr Kalam and asked him who the 'fellow' was.

He held out his index finger and thumb, about 2 inches apart, and said, 'That brown fellow.' He was slightly embarrassed to see the commotion that had ensued.

'It is a cockroach!' I exclaimed.

Dr Kalam did not like cockroaches at all. And there were some large ones in that old coach. One such fellow had crawled under his blanket. So he had hurried out of his cabin on seeing it and exclaimed in his usual manner, 'There is a fellow in there.'

The security guards, on the other hand, were confused about this missing fellow, and were too nervous to ask what he had meant.

Before they could raise an alarm, I interjected. 'You are looking for the wrong person. The fellow is little—very little.' I could not control my grin. 'It is a cockroach.'

All of us smiled at each other sheepishly. The guards were searching for the perpetrator with a gun, but perhaps a rolled-up newspaper would have been more suitable! We soon found not one, but four little brown fellows and all of them were carefully evicted from the moving train.

When we declared the cabin 'clear', Dr Kalam asked me anxiously, 'Have you thrown them out of the train?'

'But the fellows were here without a ticket!' I replied.

He smiled and went back inside.

No other fellows turned up for the rest of the journey and we reached Rourkela on time. For many days after that, I kept referring to every insect as a 'fellow' in front of Dr Kalam, and we would exchange smiles at that little joke of ours.

A Student Prayer in Kalahandi, Odisha

Dr Kalam visited some of the most remote places in Odisha. One such visit happened in the January

of 2010. We'd gone to Kalahandi for the Kalahandi
Ghumura Utsav at the Prathmik Sikshyak Bhavan,
where he met teachers, students and their parents.
To a cheering audience he said,

'When I see the students on one side, and the
teachers on the other—I look at you, dear friends,
as one integrated system of education, learning
and knowledge. The seeds of peace in the world
originate from the righteousness in the heart of
every individual. Such righteous citizens lead to
the evolution of an enlightened society. Education,
supported by a value system, has to be so designed
that righteousness is developed in young hearts. *That*
should be the mission of education.

'On this occasion, I would like to quote a
student's prayer:

"Don't impose on me what you know,
I want to explore the unknown
And be the source of my own discoveries.
Let the known be my liberation, not my slavery.
Show me so that I can stand
On your shoulders.
Reveal yourself so that I can be
Something different."'

———————— ✳ ————————

13

Make Your Mother Smile

For Dr Kalam, there was nothing and no one greater in life than one's parents, especially one's mother. He would rarely start a morning without asking me, 'You funny guy, did you speak to your mother? How is she? How is your father? Tell me.' He would insist that I speak to my parents every day, even if it was only to say hello. He would tell me, 'A few minutes of conversation over the phone will give them hours of joy,' adding, 'I spoke to my elder brother last night . . . we discussed many things. What did you discuss with your parents?' Dr Kalam's elder brother was seventeen years older than him and he had taken on the role of Dr Kalam's parents in his life.

Often during our conversations, he would say, 'Some children do not take care of their parents. Few even ill-treat them when they go out and find their own jobs and families. Parents sacrifice their lives for their children and it must be very painful for them to see their children turn their backs on them.'

More than a statement, it was a heartbreaking recollection from the accounts of his own friends and colleagues, and he tried to warn me against it. Then, to diffuse the seriousness of the discussion, he would quip, 'But I know you are not like that. You are basically a good fellow, who sometimes does funny things. But you *are* a good fellow. Tell me, are you a good fellow?'

I could only nod.

The emphasis he placed on respecting parents was a heart-warming lesson, which came up on multiple occasions.

* * *

In August 2012, on the invitation of Professor Shantaram Balwant Mujumdar, the founder of the Symbiosis Group of educational institutions, Dr Kalam visited the district of Kolhapur in Maharashtra. Kolhapur is the birthplace of Professor Mujumdar and, as an educationist, he was very passionate about the development of the area.

We specifically visited the Symbiosis School in a village called Harali, where Dr Kalam addressed a large gathering of students from that school as well as from nearby areas. The Harali school was getting a new building and the students were very excited about it. The day was extremely hot and humid. The anticipation for Dr Kalam's speech, paired with the uncomfortable weather, was making the students very restless. A loud hum filled the room.

When Dr Kalam finally came onstage to speak, the crowd fell silent. He kept his speech short, skipping many portions to make more time for questions from the audience. Just as he finished and prepared himself for the questions, I noticed a slight commotion develop amongst the crowd.

A few policemen were trying to restrain a short woman, clad in a crisp, white-pink sari. She was repeatedly saying, *'Dr Kalam se milna hai!'* (We want to meet Dr Kalam!) That was when I noticed the child she was holding. He couldn't have been more than sixteen years old. His legs had been affected by polio and they could not support him, so his mother was carrying him in her arms—as she must have done when the child was but a newborn baby. When I summoned them to the side of the stage, she said, 'My son wants to meet the Mahamahim.'[1] I asked them to wait till Dr Kalam was done with the questions from the audience and she agreed.

When the question-answer session concluded some ten minutes later, I introduced Dr Kalam to the woman and her son. This time, the young boy took over the conversation. He held out his hand and said, 'My name is Shailesh and I am from this village, Harali. You have told us to have a dream in many of your books. I am here to tell you about my dream. I am a chess player. I will work very hard and, someday, I will become a grand master'.

'Sahib,' his mother added, 'we don't need any help, just your blessings. My son always says, "If a boatman's son can

---

[1] Mahamahim means 'His Excellency' in Hindi.

become the President, your son too can become a grand master." Please bless my son, Sahib.'

Dr Kalam placed his hand on the young boy's head and said, 'You will definitely succeed. God is with you. With willpower, you can defeat any problem. But when you become a grand master, promise me that you will remember your mother's role in your journey—who has dedicated her life to fulfil your dream.'

Shailesh nodded. I could see the tears in his mother's eyes.

Later that evening, when we were flying back to Mumbai, Dr Kalam recalled the incident.

'Did you see how the mother's courage has shaped the son's dreams? Her love has given her the strength to carry the weight of a grown-up son, and the power to bear the struggle of raising a grand master in him.'

I nodded.

'That is why I say, every child should do one task every day—'

'What is that?' I interrupted.

'Make his mother smile.'

Dr Kalam always said, 'When a mother smiles, the family smiles. When families smile, the nation is happy.'

The story of the future grand master and his mother was repeated by him on numerous occasions.

* * *

Dr Kalam had delivered many speeches highlighting the necessity of bringing the youth of today closer to their mothers. His ideas on this topic finally took the shape of the 'What Can I Give' mission in 2012. In this youth-oriented movement, we worked on multiple ideas, wherein each one was targeted mainly at giving back to our families, our society and our nation. The first task for the members of this movement was to make their mothers smile every day. Dr Kalam made everyone take an oath to this effect.

We continued the mission in various parts of the nation for about one year. Through the volunteers of the What Can I Give mission, we propagated 5 lakh ideas across India on how the youth could make their mothers smile. Dr Kalam often appreciated these ideas in his speeches. At a function at the Delhi Public School, Varanasi, on 14 March 2012, Dr Kalam touched upon two such exemplary ideas. 'I have come across some touching examples and stories in the course of this mission. Let me share some of them with you.'

'Dhiraj, a tenth-standard student from Delhi wrote that a mother's love can be solved through an equation. He said,

"Mother's Love $= \text{Tan } \theta$, where $\theta = 90$ degrees."

'Hence, according to this equation, his mother's love equals infinity. What a beautiful way to express a mother's love for their child!

'Similarly, Sulochana, from the Karnataka Chapter, said that her mother was born to a very poor family and so she could only go to primary school. Her dream of getting a degree remained unfulfilled. But she wanted her two daughters to be highly educated so that they could get good jobs at big companies. She struggled very hard to convince Sulochana's father that the girls should be put in the very best school, irrespective of the expenses. She even had to fast for two or three days in defiance before Sulochana's father came around! Once he agreed to admit their daughters in a good school, she promised to never demand anything for herself. So when Sulochana got a job in a multinational company through campus placements post an engineering degree, her mother was thrilled. She was smiling through her tears as she blessed Sulochana. A daughter had finally fulfilled a mother's dreams.

Indeed, a mother's love can make her children excel in life.'

Mother

Dr Kalam wrote a beautiful poem dedicated to his mother, which, in my opinion, is one of his best.

I still remember the day when I was ten,
Sleeping on your lap to the envy of my elder
brothers and sisters.

It was a full-moon night, my world only you knew,
Mother! My Mother!
When at midnight, I woke with tears falling on my
knee
You knew the pain of your child, my Mother.
Your caring hands, tenderly removing the pain
Your love, your care, your faith gave me strength,
To face the world without fear and with
His strength.
We will meet again on the great Judgement Day.
My Mother!

—A.P.J. Abdul Kalam

———————— ✳ ————————

———————— ✳ ————————

Tolerance to Humour Is Essential for a Thinking Society

In April 2015, Vir Das, a famous comedian, made fun of Dr Kalam in his gig, enacting a hypothetical scene where a Brahmachari like him was hosting an MTV show and being attacked by some women.

We learnt from the papers that some people in the audience got so offended that they called the police. The show was disrupted and an ugly scene ensued. It was an immature act, perhaps under-rehearsed too. But nevertheless, it came from someone well-known in his field. I read about the act—and showed it to Dr Kalam the next day.

'Say, look, somebody made a joke on you and the police caught him,' I said.

'Why?' he asked.

'Because his joke was very bad,' I replied.

'Did you think it was bad?' he asked.

After explaining what the joke was, I said, 'I thought it might be offensive.'

'No, I don't agree. How can comedy of any kind be offensive? Jokes are meant to be laughed at. You smile at a joke, not the subject of the joke. Understand. That is the idea of a joke. If a joke is good, you laugh—if it is not, you don't. That's it. There is no need to feel offended. Tolerance to humour is essential for a thinking society. Now, if you didn't like it, forget the joke, let's work.'

I learnt a lesson about jokes, humour and tolerance that day.

14

Science and Spirituality

We often witness conflict between two groups of people—one that believes in science, and the other that believes in religion.

Dr Kalam was a great scientist—this is indisputable. But he was also convinced that fact and faith can together create a better planet. He once told me, 'Science and faith *must* coexist for the human good. Science provides focus—focus helps us solve questions, discover the truth and conceive inventions. Faith provides perspective—perspective helps us see how our creations and discoveries go on to impact humanity and civilization. Focus and perspective make a combination vital for the success of societies. Science accelerates progress and faith curbs it within reasonable limitations. If the two function true to their roles, they will work together for the betterment of humanity.'

Dr Kalam's own life was nourished by multiple faiths.

His father, a boatman, also served as an imam at their local mosque, and his two best friends were from two different religions—one was a Hindu and the other was a Christian. Pakshi Lakshmana Shastrigal was the head priest of the famous Rameswaram temple and a Vedic scholar, and the Reverend Father Bodal had built the first church on Rameswaram Island. Dr Kalam recalled how 'All three of them, in the unique attire of their religion, used to sit and discuss the community's problems and find solutions. Throughout the nation and the world, the need to have a frank dialogue among cultures, religions and civilizations is felt now more than ever.'

When asked where he got his humility from, Dr Kalam would always attribute it to his father. In him, he saw how simplicity and divinity could go together. Even though his father was a boatman and Dr Kalam went on to become the President of India, they shared the same values in life. Both believed that if one leads a spiritual life then that spirituality can lift them out of any kind of confusion, misery or failure.

* * *

Dr Kalam's spiritual quest was intertwined with his education. In the 1940s, he met the Reverend T.N. Sequiera, at Saint Joseph's College, as his English professor and hostel warden, along with his physics professor, Father Chinnadurai. Even at an advanced age—a week before his demise, in fact—Dr Kalam met the Reverend Chinnadurai, who was then in his nineties, to thank him for everything he had taught him.

* * *

After his education in aeronautical engineering from MIT, in the late 1950s, Dr Kalam was unable to make it into the air force as a fighter pilot. He went to Rishikesh on a trekking trip, in order to distract himself from his failure. There he met Swami Sivananda. The great seer taught the budding scientist that failures happen for a reason, and that a pure desire always leads to a positive outcome.

* * *

In the 1960s, when Dr Kalam joined ISRO, it was just a fledgling organization. His interactions with the great scientist Professor Vikram Sarabhai, and the Reverend Peter Bernard Pereira, shaped his thoughts on religion. It was here that he learnt about the true meaning of religious service. Professor Sarabhai and his team had selected a site in Thumba, Kerala, to set up their space-research facility. It was an ideal site due to its proximity to the magnetic equator. But there was a major roadblock in getting possession of the site as it was the fishing grounds of Thumba's fishermen. Moreover, it had an old church of St Mary Magdalene, a bishop's house and a school, which was under the administration of the church.

Government officials predicted that it would be impossible to relocate so many people from the site and destroy religious institutions for the sake of a space-research centre.

But upon Dr Sarabhai's persistence, it was suggested that they approach the only person who could help them in this situation—Father Pereira, the then bishop of the region.

Dr Sarabhai and Dr Kalam approached Father Pereira on a Saturday evening. The Reverend said, 'Oh Vikram, you are asking me for my children's abode, for my abode, and for God's abode. How is it possible?' Father Pereira then invited the party to visit the church on a Sunday morning. Dr Sarabhai, his team, and the forever-inquisitive disciple, Dr Kalam, took up the offer.

At church the next Sunday, the Reverend invited Dr Sarabhai up to the dais after the prayer service. Turning to everyone present, he said, 'Dear children, here is a scientist, Dr Vikram Sarabhai. What does science do for us? We benefit from the devices that science has developed to light up our homes. I am able to talk to you using this mic, thanks to technological advancement. Medical science allows doctors to diagnose and treat patients. Science and technology enhance the overall comfort and quality of human life. And what do *I* do as a preacher? I pray for you, for your well-being, and for your peace. In short, Vikram and I are doing the same job. Both science and spirituality seek the Almighty's blessings for the prosperity of the human mind and body.

'Dear children, Dr Vikram says that, within a year, he wants to build scientific facilities near the sea coast, replacing all the settlements that now stand there. Now, can you give up your abode? Can I give up my abode? Can *we* give up God's abode for such a great scientific mission?' Dr Kalam recalled how he witnessed 'a pin-drop silence for a long moment'. Then everyone got up, and the whole church reverberated with the deafening noise of a collective 'amen'.

And so work on the research centre was soon under way. But not without alternate accommodation being offered to the affected fishermen, the church and the Reverend Pereira.

* * *

Dr Kalam's life was also an example of the fact that spirituality can be found within a religion as well as without.

In the 1970s, Dr Kalam was at ISRO during a particularly crucial phase of his career. He was working on India's first SLV, which would make us the fifth country to enter space. It was then that he met Dr Brahma Prakash, director of the Vikram Sarabhai Space Centre (VSSC). VSSC, located in Thiruvananthapuram, is where ISRO manufactures most of its space vehicles.

Dr Kalam recalled Dr Prakash as being the one who taught him that tolerance of others' views and opinions is essential in the formation and functioning of teams, who accomplish tasks which are otherwise insurmountable by a lone individual. He would say, 'Dr Brahma Prakash changed the way I used to see the world. He told me once, "Kalam, if you perceive this world as mean and rude, it will disturb your concentration. The weight of our negative thoughts is equivalent to the burden of twenty bags of luggage! This excess baggage will retard your progress, and make any trip miserable."'

* * *

A few years later, in the early 1980s, Professor Satish Dhawan, the director of ISRO, under whom Dr Kalam had made his first unsuccessful launch in 1979 and then a successful one in 1980, had provided him with more soul-shaping wisdom.

One day in 2012, we were discussing the number of PhDs Dr Kalam had received. He said to me, 'Srijan, Professor Dhawan had so many master's degrees—all from the best institutions, no less—so I asked him how one can become so academically accomplished. He responded saying that academic brilliance is no different from the brilliance of a mirror, which can be diminished by a coating of dust. Only when the dust is removed, does the mirror shine and the reflection becomes clear. We can remove the impurities obscuring our souls by living pure and ethical lives, and by serving humanity. And then God will shine through us.' These words took me back to my meeting with Dr Kalam after my graduation from IIMA, in 2009. At the time, he had advised me to use my degree and gold medal to transform the society I lived in. Back in the present moment, it suddenly struck me that Dr Kalam's advice had, in fact, directly resonated from Professor Dhawan's beliefs. The more I lived and worked with Dr Kalam, the more I realized that through his words of wisdom I was getting to learn from countless great minds.

* * *

In the 1990s, Dr Kalam met Jain muni Acharya Mahapragya, the tenth head of the Svetambar Terapanth order of Jainism. The great spiritual guru taught Dr Kalam that 'our consciousness is the birthplace of our ethics'. Recalling the Jain muni, Dr Kalam once said, 'He taught me that we instinctively *know* what is right when our conscience is clear. Our conscience is our true friend.'

* * *

In 2001, Dr Kalam met Pramukh Swamiji, the spiritual head of Shri Swaminarayan Sanstha. Their interaction prompted Dr Kalam to believe that life can have no foundation unless we recognize that an eternal spirit is the inhabitant of each individual living body. This means that everything on this planet, every species of life—including vegetation and the minerals—is a different form of one great spirit. And if everything is one spirit, then how can we ensure that one of us doesn't suffer at the hands of another? How can we help the poor? His deep respect for Pramukh Swamiji led him to write a book on him in 2015, fourteen years after their first meeting. This lesson also inspired him to work on his grandest development plan—PURA. The project aimed to provide the best services and amenities to the most marginalized people of the nation and the world. The very same idea inspired Dr Kalam and me to write our first book together, *Target 3 Billion* (2011).

* * *

Later in the 2000s, when Dr Kalam met Dadi Prakashmaniji of the Brahma Kumaris, she gave him a unique perspective. She said that silence is the unifying factor between science and spirituality, and that the aim of both the scientific and the spiritual approach is the establishment of truth. In 2007, when Dadi passed away at the age of eighty-seven years, Dr Kalam recalled her immortal thoughts in a message, 'Science approaches problems through experimental means while spirituality approaches them through experiential learning. In order to establish the truth, both approaches need to watch the process silently, without creating any turbulence.' Dr Kalam's veneration for silence guided his thinking and his way of life. Silent contemplation was his chosen method of addressing any complex issue. Later, he attended many events of the Brahma Kumaris, to deepen his own understanding and, during such sessions, he also shared his own lessons with them.

One evening in 2011, a few of the Brahma Kumari spiritual leaders, addressed as 'sisters', came to meet him at his office at 10, Rajaji Marg. I had the chance to usher them into the meeting room and exchange a few quick words. At dinner that night, I asked Dr Kalam about the meeting. He replied, 'They have a civilization of harmony. Everyone is called brother and sister, uniting the world into a single family. It is remarkable that the organization of millions is led by dadis,[1] all of whom are women. Perhaps, only women can have such intensely compassionate souls, which radiates kindness like gravity, drawing people together. Only a powerful soul can offer love and be humble. If we are weak, we become selfish; if we are empty, we take; if we are filled, we automatically give to all. That is our nature. That is the nature of the Brahma Kumaris.'

* * *

---

[1] 'Dadi' means 'grandmother' in Hindi.

In April 2009, Dr Kalam was invited to attend the 102nd birthday celebrations of His Holiness Dr Sri Sri Shivakumara Mahaswamiji in the Tumkur district of Karnataka. Mahaswamiji is a remarkable person, who has dedicated his life to the service of humanity. His greatest contribution is the establishment of a free residential education system for more than nine thousand children in the ashram. The most astonishing aspect of the entire event of his birthday was that the 102-year-old Swamiji stood on his feet without any support! He looked as steady and alert as any other youngster present there. This display of inner strength touched Dr Kalam deeply.

A couple of days later, we were discussing this unusual birthday party. I said to him, 'Sir, do you know, only four out of 1 lakh people cross the age of 100?' I had googled the subject beforehand. He replied, 'But how many of these four would be able to stand tall for half an hour, give a wise discourse, and then go on to feed thousands of children?' Of course nobody could know the exact answer to this question but the question itself led to many other relevant queries. 'I wonder what powers Mahaswamiji possesses that keep him so strong at such an advanced age? Maybe it's a balanced diet and a healthy lifestyle, or perhaps it's genetics?' I asked.

Dr Kalam sat contemplating deeply.

He recollected the tenet of goodness of action from Pramukh Swamiji. Then, perhaps swimming in silence to the shores of Mahapragyaji, he gathered the sands of conscience to be our guide, our best friend. Deeper down in the space-time of memory, he must have heard Professor Brahma Prakash's words about the need of living a pure and ethical life, and Father Pereira's and Dr Sarabhai's lesson of selflessness in service. Eventually his thoughts would have settled on Swami Sivananda of Rishikesh, in whom he saw great tranquility, and finally they must have come full circle with the memory of the life of simplicity of his father, who always espoused the value of giving back.

At long last, he spoke. 'It is the very spirit of What Can I Give.' He elaborated, 'Mahaswamiji lives with the beliefs and ethos of our mission. He gives and gives—education to famished minds, food to famished bodies. In giving so much, he becomes strong. His munificence fuels his strength. That is what keeps him standing tall and active in life. The essence of a happy life and a peaceful society lies in one sentence—*What can I give?*'

Turning to me, he asked, 'What is the reverse of "what can I give"?'

Circumspectly I replied, 'What can I . . . take?'

'Yes,' he said, 'and that is the thought which is responsible for all the wrong we see around us. We think that we can take from the environment and destroy it indiscriminately; we think of what we can take from other humans, leading us to corruption and inequity. This attitude of taking and taking even destroys families. To keep this planet liveable and the human race thriving, we have to replace this attitude of "what can I take" with the goodness of "what can I give".'

The gravity of the message struck me. This challenge became my silent motivation.

Three years later, in 2012, this idea became a reality as our What Can I Give movement, through which Dr Kalam tried to combat corruption, environmental degradation and social evils.

It is important that we ask ourselves this question, for in the answer lies the truth of humanity. So go ahead and question yourself.

What can I give?

The answers will be astounding.

The What Can I Give Auto

In November 2011, Dr Kalam and I encountered something unusual on our way to 10, Rajaji Marg from the Delhi airport. It was around 6.30 p.m., the sky was getting darker and the traffic thicker by the minute. Our convoy consisted of only two cars, led by a police jeep. We were about to reach our destination when we drove past an autorickshaw. I saw a large sign stuck to the back of the vehicle:

Gareebo aur bimmaron ke liye aadha kiraya (50% discount for sick and poor people)

I immediately pointed it out to Dr Kalam but by then we had whizzed past the auto. He replied, 'Oh. He is the Giving Auto. He radiates the message of What Can I Give. I am touched by his compassion. I would like to meet this benevolent man.'

We could not halt our convoy right then as it would have led to a traffic jam but when we reached home, I decided to go out on my motorbike and try to find the Giving Auto. The chances of finding the vehicle and its driver were slim, but it was worth a shot.

Of course I could not find the Giving Auto. But the memory of it persisted with the both of us. It reaffirmed what Dr Kalam often said, 'To be a giver, you don't need to be rich. All you need is compassion in your heart and a smile on your face.'

15

If You Consume from the Past, You Owe a Debt to the Future

In November 2010, I found an unexpected mail in Dr Kalam's official mailbox. It was from a famous author, Howard Bloom. To be honest, I had not heard of him till then, but his email signature mentioned the books he had written, the most prominent being *The Genius of the Beast*. I proceeded to do a quick Google search, and was stunned by what I found.

Howard Bloom's life was an inspiration in itself. In 1988, he became disabled due to chronic fatigue syndrome. A person with this condition often suffers from bouts of extreme fatigue and exhaustion, for no apparent reason, and sometimes these spells may last for over twenty-four hours. In Mr Bloom's case, this condition forced him to leave his strenuous job, after which he tried his hand at multiple careers. Since the diagnosis, he had published three books on human evolution and group behaviour.

After a remarkable switch in career paths at the age of forty-five, Howard had become an advocate for investments into futuristic science. Then I stumbled upon a very interesting fact—Howard Bloom was also the former publicist of Billy Joel, one of my favourite singers. The mail we had received was interesting too.

It discussed some preliminary aspects of a new form of energy known as Space-based Solar Power (SBSP). In his email, Mr Bloom urged Dr Kalam to lead the campaign globally and said that he was willing to connect the dots across the world to make this a reality. It was a bold, futuristic and improbable idea, but don't all great inventions begin with an incredible proposal?

I took a printout of the mail and showed it to Dr Kalam, who was immediately attracted to the concept. He was drawn by the sheer scope, the near-impossibility and the absolute novelty of the suggestion. We immediately decided to embark on this challenge. Thus began our long research into this new form of generating energy from space. For the next five years, and till the end of his life, Dr Kalam remained an ardent advocate and researcher of this topic.

We wrote back to Mr Bloom about our inclination and enthusiasm, who then contacted other scientists, such as John Mankin and Mark Hopkins, for this project. Soon, the National Space Society (NSS) of the US and ISRO came on board as well. Thus, by the end of 2010, within weeks of our first email exchange, the Kalam-NSS Energy Initiative was launched on a global scale. It was rolled out at a remarkable speed, considering that the involved organizations and people were scattered all over the planet.

Today, Space Solar Power, or SSP as it is better known as, is a wonderful opportunity for humankind and yet, a great challenge. There is no doubt that, in the years to come, land will become a scarce resource. This makes it imperative for mankind to start searching for new sources of energy available in outer space. SSP is quite an exciting proposition in theory because the amount and energy of sunlight available in space is much higher than that available on the surface of the earth, given the absence of protective atmospheric layers in space. Moreover, such a technology might be of special interest to future generations, who could even reside in outer space!

We went through almost all the available data and publications on this subject. And, after discussions with experts from around the globe, we estimated that SSP would yield almost twice the amount of power than what is generated by a terrestrial or a land-based solar-power system now. Our counterparts in the US agreed to it.

Of course, the greatest challenge was to direct electricity from a space station on to the surface of the earth. Would laser beams be better suited for this purpose or microwaves? Dr Kalam suggested a completely new dimension—nano-robots. Nano-robots are extremely small, about one-billionth of a millimeter in size. They can carry energy back and forth between the earth's surface and the space station. They are as fine as dust particles, and capable of floating back into space using minimal energy. Although the concept of nano-robots sounds impossible, they do exist in real life. Nano-robots are already being used for the purpose of drug delivery to organs inside the human body. And there is no reason why this same technology can't be used for delivering energy from space.

We found another obstacle to the SSP dream, which to me was slightly depressing. Given our current state of technological progress, SSP, even in its nascent form, was at least fifty years away. In fact, SSP at an optimal scale is perhaps not possible before the year 2075. Despite the awareness of this fact, Dr Kalam pushed the subject at various forums, one of them being the China Energy and Environment Summit (CEES) in 2011.

One day, while we were working on Dr Kalam's CEES speech, I said to him, 'Sir, this project will take at least fifty to sixty years to come to fruition. Why do you want to invest your efforts into this? None of us will be alive to see this happen. It is beyond our lifetime.'

In all honesty, it was just a casual remark, albeit with a hint of pessimism. It originated from the basic human desire to reap the benefits of our hard work. We want to see the results of our efforts within our lifetime. But this statement did not go down well with my ever-optimistic teacher.

He immediately replied, 'Look at the tree,' pointing at a mango tree, which was visible from the little window behind me. I turned around to look at it.

'Some fellow must have planted it years ago. Maybe it never bore a single fruit for a decade. Perhaps, the person who sowed the seed, watered the plant and protected it, did not get to taste a single mango from the tree. But he trusted that the mangoes, whenever they appeared on his tree, would be sweet. Today, we are enjoying the fruits of the tree, without even knowing the name of the person who has made it possible. It was his selfless faith and unflinching trust that has made our day.'

I did not expect this reaction, but it made sense.

He continued, 'I can tell you one thing—this is the trajectory of science and progress. The guy who discovered electricity never saw a ray of light. I am sure he knew that he himself would never see any benefit from his invention, but that did not hamper his commitment towards the project. Srijan, we are all links in a continuous chain of evolution and development. Great scientists will come and go, and add some incremental knowledge that will be of use to us, long after they have turned to dust. Their lives are sacrificed for works whose fruits are borne after their lifetimes. This is what the Gita says, doesn't it?'

I nodded, recalling the verses where Lord Krishna reminds Arjuna about the fact that the warriors on the battlefield of Kurukshetra were indeed indestructible and that they would exist timelessly. In Chapter 2 Verse 12 of the Bhagavad Gita, Krishna says, 'In fact, there was never a time when I did not exist, nor did you, nor did these kings; and never shall we all cease to exist hereafter.'

Dr Kalam concluded, 'We consume so much so easily, and often so thoughtlessly from our past. This bulb, this computer, this electricity, the fruits and the food that we eat are the results of hard work derived from history.

'Success often comes as an unplanned by-product when you mix purpose, hard work and perseverance. When you consume from history, you owe the future. This project of SSP is our repayment for the debt that we owe our past generations. We stand on the shoulders of giants who came before us, and we need to raise the bar higher and leave something better behind us. This is how humankind progresses. I will surely not see it becoming a reality in my lifetime, but I know it will be a reality *someday*. The fruits of our efforts, whenever they appear, shall be sweet.'

And then, to temper the seriousness of it all, he said, 'Watch out, I say! *You* will surely live to see it in *your* lifetime. Just be careful of your health . . .'

After a moment's pause he passed me a platter of fruits. 'Here, have these apples. They are good for health and will give you a longer life.'

I smiled. Hopefully, SSP would someday bear sweet fruits for all of humankind, even if I am not there to witness it. But it sure would be nice if it happens in my lifetime.

16

Heed the Voice of the Grass Roots

The year 2011 was monumental for the Indian democracy.

In the months preceding 2011, India was rocked by some of the most astounding large-scale allegations of corruption in business, politics, bureaucracy and governance. It was becoming evident that this menace had reached the level of organized, insidious crime. Some of the biggest cases were the 2011 Commonwealth Games scandal, the Adarsh Housing Society scam, the 2010 housing loan scam, the Radia tapes controversy and the 2G spectrum scam. The nation was losing all faith in the system of governance, and the citizens were getting angry.

I was just twenty-six years old then, and at the time living in Delhi was like living in the eye of the storm. In the first few months of 2011, all the resentment against corruption was culminating in the form of protests. This was also the time when many prominent members of the civil society, such as Kiran Bedi, Ramdev, Swami Agnivesh and others, approached Dr Kalam individually and collectively, requesting him to participate in a movement that they were planning. They wanted to hold street protests in order to advocate the introduction of the Jan Lokpal Bill, which they believed would go a long way in solving the problem of corruption.

Not far from 10, Rajaji Marg, at Jantar Mantar and then at India Gate, I witnessed protest after protest being held against the evils of fraud and black money. Like many others in Delhi, and all over India, I too had been affected by this issue, and could empathize with these movements.

In June 2011, things went from bad to ugly to violent when Baba Ramdev's agitation against black money at the Ramlila Ground was met with police action. More than fifty people were injured. Baba Ramdev himself was detained after he tried to escape unsuccessfully in camouflage, dressed as a woman. That was when I started asking Dr Kalam what *he* thought about this problem, which, I believed, was extremely shameful for the entire nation.

After the incident at Ramlila Ground, I asked him, 'What is your opinion on these incidents?'

He took a deep breath and said, 'Governments need to be more patient with the people. Sometimes when people get the power to fly high, they lose the ability to listen to voices from the ground.' I was not happy with this answer, and so I probed further. 'You are the former President of India and are known as the People's President. So what is the People's President going to do about this situation? *Your* people are in trouble.'

He sensed the urgency in my tone.

'Look,' he said, 'I believe corruption is a cancer which is indeed affecting our nation. I know that drastic action is needed to remove this disease. Do you think one new institution is enough to solve corruption?' He was referring to the much debated Jan Lokpal Bill.

'Lokpal, even at its best, might send just a few more corrupt people to jail. Which is fine. But we need *more*. We need to eliminate corruption from every household, and from the human character itself. We need citizens who will put the nation above the rest. The movement has to begin within every person, every family, and then it has to spread to the schools. It has to work towards reforming the generation and it has to create a new meaning of citizenship. To win against corruption, we need strategic thinking, a system reboot—that should begin at home and spread across the nation.'

Dr Kalam always gave me the liberty to be candid—after all, he was my teacher. Perhaps I even used to misuse the freedom a little. I asked, 'What will *you* do in all this? And when?'

He sensed the undertone of a challenge in my question and said, 'Soon. And there *will* be a moment. You just watch.'

And indeed, there was such a moment.

A few months later, in 2012, we finally developed the idea of launching Dr Kalam's own movement—the What Can I Give movement. As discussed, the central idea of the mission was to do away with the concept of 'what can I take', which we believed was the sole reason for the existence of corruption.

Dr Kalam urged all the young participants of the movement to talk to their parents, especially their fathers, and make them understand that moderate consumption was the key. We all believed that this message of concern, coming from the children, would awaken the deficit conscience in the minds of their parents.

The path that we chose to combat corruption is open to support as well as doubt, but we can all agree on the fact that Dr Kalam liked to uproot every problem from its very base. Throughout his life, he considered people as essentially compassionate beings, who are filled with emotions and complexities, and who *have* the ability to make good judgements. Therefore he always came up with sustainable solutions that had deeper impacts in the future. The solution that we found for the menace of corruption in our What Can I Give mission was simple, but well-researched. It was based on our core human values and addressed the root cause of the moral turpitude prevalent in society. This ability to find a simple answer to a complex problem was the hallmark of Dr Kalam.

17

The Presidential Elections, 2012

One of the most tense yet exciting periods that I have spent with Dr Kalam came unannounced in the summer of 2012.

Smt. Pratibha Patil was on the verge of retiring from the highest office of the nation, and the election for the 12th President of India was scheduled to be held on 19 July 2012. In India, the presidential elections are conducted through a process of indirect voting, wherein the MPs and the MLAs cast votes for their favourite presidential candidate. Back then, the ruling United Progressive Alliance (UPA) government, led by the Indian National Congress (INC), had a clear majority in choosing the next President.

By the end of April, the Bharatiya Janata Party (BJP), the opposition party, announced that they wanted to put up a candidate of their own.

As the day of the election drew closer, the media went into a frenzy, trying to predict who the next President would be. Of course, the presidential elections in India are indirect, with only sitting MPs and MLAs being allowed to vote. The media, on the other hand, went on a different tangent; they started conducting surveys to find out which candidate was most popular among the citizens. The results of these surveys started getting published. Dr Kalam's name surfaced at the top of every single survey.

On 13 June 2012, the Chief Minister of West Bengal, Mamata Banerjee met Congress president, Sonia Gandhi to discuss her choice for the new President. Soon after the meeting, Mamata Banerjee spoke candidly to the media and disclosed, 'Soniaji's first choice is Shri Pranab Mukherjee and her second choice is Shri Hamid Ansari.' The media was confused as to why she had two choices in mind instead of having one clear candidate. Within a couple of hours, Mamata Banerjee and Shri Mulayam Singh, chief of the Samajwadi Party, addressed a joint press conference where they declared, 'Our choices are Dr A.P.J. Abdul Kalam or Dr Manmohan Singh or Shri Somnath Chatterjee.'

The long-simmering presidential race was now on fire.

Though the speed at which the events were unfolding surprised us, the events themselves did not. Some of the senior leaders had already been asking Dr Kalam if he was willing to take on the presidential position again. Since he had dropped out of the presidential race in 2007, the political class was unsure of whether he would contest at all in 2012.

The support from Mamata Banerjee and Mulayam Singh soon gave the BJP its choice of candidate, whom they could pitch against any UPA candidate. The Congress, the leading party of UPA, was visibly shocked because Mamata Banerjee had disclosed the discussion that she'd had with Mrs Gandhi. They quickly gathered consensus and decided on a single name—Shri Pranab Mukherjee. Pranab Mukherjee was accepted by almost everyone. He was the ruling party's best chance at keeping smaller ally parties from swinging away into supporting Dr Kalam's candidacy, should a contest happen. But both the BJP's hopes and the Congress's fear hinged on one key question—would Dr Kalam actually contest for the post?

If he did contest, there was a likelihood of him losing the elections and, moreover, he had already forgone the opportunity to do the same in 2007.

The next day, we were scheduled to go to Patna for the launch of Dr Kalam's What Can I Give initiative in Bihar. In those delicate times, every moment was important. Since this particular event was organized solely by my team, the first thing I suggested to Dr Kalam the night before 14 June was—

'Sir, let me postpone this event. We can do it later. Right now, we should stay in Delhi and monitor the situation.'

'Who have you called as the audience?'

'Sir, about six hundred school children and some parents from Bihar.'

'So why should *they* suffer because we have some funny events going on here? They are good guys, they are young, and they are on a mission to work for the nation and eradicate corruption. My first duty is to attend to *them*, before I do anything for politics. Forget all this for one day; we must fulfil our responsibility first. Let us go through my lecture now.'

Earlier that day, the media had gathered outside Dr Kalam's house. There was a frenzy of activity—journalists jostling against each other, OB vans honking. Dr Kalam and I were taking a walk around the garden that evening—he was the picture of calm, despite the obtrusive antennas of the vans peeking above the wall.

I urged him again. 'Sir, you should consider delaying. Look at all these people—the general public, other than the media personnel. They are also waiting to hear from you.'

He replied, 'Let me tell you a story. Do you know the great teacher and scientist C.V. Raman?'

I nodded and said, 'Of course.'

'When C.V. Raman was conferred the Bharat Ratna in 1954, he got a telegram asking him to report to the Rashtrapati Bhavan on a particular date. Of course, getting the Bharat Ratna was a big thing but the date of invitation worried Raman. He pondered over it for a few hours and then wrote a letter, expressing his inability to go receive the award.'

I did not know this story. 'Really? Why?'

'Think of what could have been more important to him than the highest award of the nation . . . Raman politely apologized in his letter and stated that he could not attend the event on the mentioned date, because on that very day his research student was supposed to deliver his final presentation. He said, "My student needs me. He has worked hard on his thesis for many years. I cannot let *him* down for *my* award." Raman found it unbecoming of a teacher to put his personal benefits above his professional commitment to a student. Of course, the award ceremony was shifted to another date.

'Those students in Patna have followed our mission, and have walked on a difficult path in the current times. I cannot let them down. They are *our* students.'

We made a few short calls to friends and long-time colleagues of Dr Kalam, asking for their opinion. That was all. Everything else was pushed aside, to be dealt with after the Patna event.

On the evening of 14 June, when we were in Patna, the CM of Bihar, Shri Nitish Kumar came to meet Dr Kalam. He too was curious to know if Dr Kalam would contest for the presidential post. Minutes later, the press asked the same question. Dr Kalam clearly had not put much thought into it, and said, 'Wait and watch. I will decide at the right time.'

This puzzling statement set off a fresh round of speculations.

When we returned to Delhi the next day, things became even more tense. We summoned many people to the office, and that day our little room was buzzing with opinions and ideas. Out of the ten people present in the room, only two were of the opinion that Dr Kalam should contest again—I was one of them. But the rest were either sceptical or completely opposed to the idea. The evening ended without any concrete decisions.

On the morning of 16 June, the third day since the drama had begun to escalate, we heard from the BJP president, L.K. Advani. His ambassador, Sudheerandra Kulkarni, told us, 'Advaniji has spoken to all our CMs. Everyone wants to see you contest. It is a unanimous decision.'

While the BJP was still awaiting Dr Kalam's approval, the RSS chief, Shri Mohan Bhagwat, openly declared their support for him on the 17th.

The situation intensified even further on 18 June.

Advaniji called personally and said that he was willing to go on a national campaign to garner support for Dr Kalam, if the latter agreed to contest. Everybody, including those openly supporting Dr Kalam, knew that the numbers were stacked oddly against him. Media polls were also in agreement with this assessment. With the Congress party against him, and the UPA having a clear majority in both houses and in most of the state assemblies, the highest percentage of votes that Dr Kalam could get was just 42 per cent. The media opined that Dr Kalam could win only if he promoted cross-voting within all the parties. Many media experts believed that with Dr Kalam's popularity, it was likely for the MPs and MLAs to cross-vote. But we, his close associates, knew that he would never encourage the petty politics of cross-voting. In reality, we also knew that there was no chance of Dr Kalam winning the elections. He might have been the unanimous winner in the hearts of the people, but politicians were a different group altogether.

Under ordinary circumstances, he would have repeated what he did in 2007 and withdrawn from this contest—then what made him ponder over this decision for almost a week?

While Advaniji was cautious, Mamata Banerjee was more emotional in her appeals. She even started her own social media channel to muster popular support for Dr Kalam.

But we soon found out that Dr Kalam was reluctant to contest for the post.

He personally rang her to tell her about his intention to withdraw from the contest. Overwhelmed by his answer, she replied, 'Sir! I am a politician. It will be a rare opportunity in my career if I can do such a great deed for the nation. This is my opportunity to serve the nation by bringing you back to the Rashtrapati Bhavan. The nation needs you and I am willing to put my career at stake to do something so great for India. Please help us and support us. Let me do my best for the nation.'

After the conversation, Dr Kalam sat by the phone, visibly moved. For once, his confidence in his own decision had been shaken. Dr Kalam had had very little to do with Mamata Banerjee in the past, and this surge of respect from her was unexpected and touching. Her emotional appeals were indeed a major factor in Dr Kalam still considering the race.

But the primary reason behind Dr Kalam's hesitation in pulling out of this sure loss was something else.

It was because the People's President so greatly wished to fight corruption at the grass roots of the nation. Our discussion had taken a new angle—even if Dr Kalam fought a losing election, could he help awaken the nation against corruption and win the battle against this cancer? It was only then I realized how deeply disturbed he was by the rampant corruption cases—tumbling one after another and tirelessly gnawing away at Dr Kalam's dream of India 2020. I saw his hidden anger, and not just his disappointment, at the cancer of corruption.

Of course, except the two people in the office, nobody agreed on this extraordinary idea of running for the presidential post which was already lost. One after the other, senior advisers and friends came up with reasons as to why Dr Kalam should simply bow out of the race. They saw little outcome or merit in this whole plan of spreading a positive word for a corruption-free India. While they did see merit in the intention, few saw it working out into anything substantial.

'Your last coordinate in history will be of someone who *lost* the thirteenth presidential elections,' said one of the senior colleagues. 'That's how your Wikipedia page will read,' added another.

'But history will also remember you as someone who fought the battle against corruption for the sake of the nation's future—even at the cost of losing some points on the scorecard of history,' I retorted.

Personally, back then I believed, and I still do, that if Dr Kalam had contested in 2012, he would have lost the elections by a narrow margin. But in that one month between 18 June and 19 July, when the voting took place, he could have triggered a new revolution among the nation's youth, urging them to stand tall and firm against corruption and ask the 'system' to give way to the idea of India 2020. It would have been the reboot that the nation needed. With the strength of Dr Kalam's What Can I Give mission, we could have harnessed the youth's anger into positive action for the country. A part of Dr Kalam's thoughts echoed with this belief, and that kept him floating in the race which he otherwise would have rejected on the very first day.

Later that week, after most of the people had left office, Dr Kalam asked us to retrieve a photo of him signing the papers for the presidential elections in 2002. And we found it.

'What do you see?' he asked us.

'I see you. There is Vajpayeeji on your right . . .' I said.

He stopped me. 'No! You are a funny fellow. I asked you *what* you see and you are telling me *who* you see.'

I still did not understand the question. Confused, I blabbered on, 'I see a table, some chairs, and some people sitting around . . .'

He laughed aloud. I stopped and gave up.

'See, there is togetherness in this picture. All the opposing politicians have come together for a unique occasion. It is rare. It is beautiful. This is how things should work out. Don't you think if I contest now then I will become a point of division?' he said gently.

Even though he had a valid argument, I was determined to convince him to stand for the elections.

'Sir, but what about the people of the nation, all of whom want you to contest? And if you don't fear defeat, then why don't you contest and use this as an opportunity to galvanize the nation on critical issues like corruption, education, harmony, and, above all, the idea of the nation as a whole?'

He then said, 'Let us see. But we must not keep the media people waiting. It must be difficult for them to keep standing outside. They have been there all day and all night.'

This was the end of our conversation and soon Dr Kalam set out for a short walk in the garden. My heart still wanted him to undertake this mission, but I could sense his answer now. As a last attempt, my colleague—the only other supporter for Dr Kalam contesting—and I sat down and composed two letters. One was meant for the occasion if Dr Kalam chose to contest and the other if he chose not to. Taking printouts of the two letters, I went to look for him.

I found Dr Kalam at the entrance of the main building. He was latching the door. I told him, 'Sir, choose whichever letter you like. Now I will learn about your decision only from the media tomorrow morning.'

'Let me think about it. But before you leave, get something packed for dinner—it is late.' It was indeed past midnight.

The next morning I rushed to the office. There was a huge crowd outside his house, all waiting in anticipation of the big news. Inside, the secretaries were already busy taking photocopies. I saw that they weren't using any staplers to put the pages together, which could only mean one thing—he had chosen the shorter note. He was not going to contest.

I did not feel like being a part of this dead end and so I went upstairs to the smaller office. A secretary approached me. 'Sahib wants to talk to you.'

I was dejected. What was left to discuss now, I wondered. I dragged myself to his reading room, which was across the library. He was sitting there with his breakfast.

He stopped eating when he saw me and said, 'I don't want to be a point of division. I have thought about it. It is better to let the politicians come together than to let them move apart. We will go ahead with the mission anyway. It may take a little more time—but then we have time, don't we?'

He spoke apologetically, 'I know you have done a lot of hard work and spent long days and nights working on this. I am thankful to you for that.'

He then asked me to shut the door, which I had left open behind me. As soon as I did as instructed, he continued, 'Look, I know you are angry about this. You can yell at me. I give you ten minutes. Nobody will come till then. Go ahead.'

Of course, I could never yell at Dr Kalam. All I could say was, 'Now that you have decided, we will stick to your decision.'

We both smiled. Then he said, 'I have one more work for you. We must thank the people who supported us despite the odds. Let us draft a letter first to Mamataji.'

✳

Letter of Thanks

The letter addressed to Mamata Banerjee was posted on social media via Facebook.

Dear and Respected Mamataji,
May I thank you for proposing my name for the presidential elections of 2012 and for all your ceaseless efforts?

During our short interaction, I saw in you a great leadership quality of 'graceful politics'. Your firmness for a cause, honesty for the cause of the nation, and particularly your courage and determination to sacrifice the golden throne of politics, is indeed graceful politics. This is indeed the need of the country. It is known that history is written only by courageous leaders.

I am extremely sorry for the disappointment I have caused you.

With kind regards,

Yours sincerely,

A.P.J. Abdul Kalam

I was surprised by the apology in the last line. I asked him why he had mentioned it, and what he was sorry about.

His reply was simple.

'We are disappointing those who were standing for us, even when the tides were against us. We must apologize for the exit.'

We will never get to know how Dr Kalam would have managed his second term if he had won, given that he had prior experience of being the President. We will also never get to know what sort of a national uprising he could have roused if he had actually contested.

This episode made me respect my teacher all the more and also gave us some new ideas, which we implemented in the What Can I Give mission throughout 2012.

If Contesting
Address to the Nation

My dear people,

You are aware of the developments in the run-up to the presidential elections. Though I have never aspired to serve another term or showed interest in contesting the elections, some political parties wanted me to be their candidate. Many citizens have also expressed the same wish. It only reflects their love and affection for me and the aspiration of the people. I'm really overwhelmed by this support. This being their wish, I respect it. I want to thank them for the trust they have in me.

My dear fellow Indians, I know millions and millions of you want me to become the President again. I am aware of your sentiments—of the many emails, calls, messages signature campaigns, meetings, and comments on websites expressing your support for me. Many political parties approached me, requesting to contest the elections. But I have always believed that the President of India should emerge as a consensus candidate. There should be no races leading to the Rashtrapati Bhavan.

The first citizen should be above politics and political ideologies. Even when major political parties proposed me as their candidate in 2007, I made it clear that there should be no contest. Being the serving President or former President makes little difference to me. I think I am freer now to meet the youth of this country and listen to their ideas. In the last five years, I've met millions of children across the country and shared my thoughts with them.

The Trinamool Congress (TMC) and NDA leaders called me to say that I should contest in this election. There is pressure from all corners in this regard. Some friends are saying that I should not contest and continue with my duties gracefully. A majority, however, wants me to contest this election for two reasons—to honour the desires of a large number of people, particularly that of the youth, and to respect the political parties that have reposed faith in me. So, my friends, what is my duty and how do I honour the will of the 1.2 billion people of the nation?

My dear people, I consider my life an open book. The views of the common man have always played a key role in my decision-making, even on the personal front. Now, my fellow citizens, we together have to collectively decide whether WE should contest or not. Yes, we know the numbers are not favourable.

The political parties who want me as their candidate know this fact as well. The people also know that I may not win if I contest.

But, after giving a thought to all this, I think, that we will lose even if we don't contest. I will be a loser, having let down the parties that pinned their hopes on me. I will be a loser, having let down the desires and sentiments of a majority of Indians, including the millions of students and NRIs who have conveyed their support. I am made to think that I am more the people's candidate.

Today, India stands at a moment of transition, which rarely occurs in the lifetime of a nation. On one hand, we have the strength of 60 crore youth, and on the other hand, we have even more people below the poverty line to cater to. On one hand, we have the hardworking middle class leading the growth of the economy by their sweat and blood, and on the other hand, we have a few corrupt leaders who are wiping the entire effort of the workforce in one stroke of scam—which runs into astounding numbers of lakhs of crores! We have Indians who are controlling businesses internationally, but we also have reputed international agencies that are pointing out how a lot is lacking in our domestic politics. Why are we said to be a nation of first-rate citizens governed by a third-rate governance system?

Where we go from this transition . . . whether we fly, we walk or we fall . . . is in our hands.

It also occurs to me that the people and the political parties want a worthy change. They seem to be frustrated with certain developments in the recent past that have questioned the very credibility and fundamentals of the Constitution, as well as certain rights guaranteed therein. We have only eight years to make this country a developed country before 2020. But we are lacking in all fronts—economy, societal upliftment from poverty, freedom from corruption, moral turpitude, curbing black money, price control of essential commodities, putting a stop to horse trading for the sake of political gain, good management of our external affairs and its strategy, a degree of confidence in India by our neighbours, prompt redressal of human-rights violations, an overall climate of peace. Instead of progressing along the path, our country is but derailing.

Perhaps they are looking to bring about a change by nominating me. The same people showed their solidarity towards recent anti-corruption movements. With a small team, civic societies emerged from nowhere and the whole nation followed the mission. At every given opportunity, Indians have shown their anger against the flaws in the system, which they think need immediate rectification.

Contesting this election will be a win-win situation for me. If I lose the election, I still win because I honoured the views of millions and millions of people. If I do win, the people win, as the campaign for change—orchestrated by you—wins. So my dear Indians, I have decided to contest this election with ALL OF YOU. I enter the fray knowing well that the numbers are against me. I will contest knowing well that I lack the majority. I will run the race knowing well that I will lose. But I have already won in the hearts of the people and I am now duty-bound to contest this election for them.

I don't belong to any political party. I neither endorse nor oppose any political ideology. I am just a scientist and I always wish to be remembered as a teacher. Now that I have decided to face the elections, I have become a candidate. A candidate has to campaign in an election by meeting party leaders and seeking their support. I don't have a party or cadre-strength to campaign or lobby for votes. I appeal to *you*, my dear Indians, to campaign for me.

Friends, at eighty years of age, having served as a President already, I have no complaints losing an election—as long as we can all awaken. Awaken together for a better, economically developed, socially equitable and corruption-free India where the nation is above any party, any organization or any individual. Where narrow fences of division do not hold us from coming together to transform the nation. Can all this happen? Will you help me achieve this?

I have realized that my decision to contest this election is our collective decision. I am the people's candidate now. I hope you will continue to shower the same love on me whether I win or lose. Maybe I am bound to lose—I don't know. But I am certainly bound to be true, loyal and affectionate to you. This is not a political statement or campaign mantra. But a few words that come straight from my heart.

Let me conclude with a verse from the Bhagavad Gita:

'karmany evadhikaras te
ma phalesu kadachana
ma karma-phala-hetur bhur
ma te sango'stv akarmani'

('You have a right to perform your prescribed duty, but you are not entitled to the fruits of action. Never consider yourself the cause of the results of your activities, and never be attached to not doing your duty.')

God bless you, my dear people.

Jai Hind.

If Not Contesting
Address to the Nation

My dear friends,

You are aware of the developments in the run-up to the presidential elections. Though I have never aspired to serve another term or showed interest in contesting the elections, TMC chief Mamata Banerjee and other political parties wanted me to be their candidate. Many, many citizens have also expressed the same wish. It only reflects their love and affection for me and the aspiration of the people. I'm really overwhelmed by this support. This being their wish, I respect it. I want to thank them for the trust they have in me.

I have considered the totality of the matter. Considering the present political situation, I have decided not to contest the presidential elections.

May God bless you all.

18

Intelligence Is beyond Education

In March 2012, Dr Kalam visited the remote district of Jaunpur in eastern Uttar Pradesh. Jaunpur is a relatively arid region and, in the month of March, it witnesses significant temperature variations from day to night.

The main reason behind the visit was a small school called Sujanganj Pranavam Intermediate School. It was a low-income educational institution run by a couple who had migrated from Kerala two decades ago. They had learnt the local language and had dedicated their lives to the cause of education. The spirit of service had brought the couple to the dry, dusty city of Jaunpur, a thousand miles away from their home. They had built their school in the middle of the wheat farms in the city.

A few months ago, the couple had visited Dr Kalam's house in Delhi. He was so thrilled to hear their story that he had promptly arranged a visit to Jaunpur. In many ways, he could relate it to his own childhood when he received an education amidst economic difficulties.

Jaunpur is not connected by air from Delhi, and the nearest airports are located in Allahabad and Varanasi. These places are quite far away from the village and Dr Kalam always insisted on travelling by standard commercial airlines only, as he never wanted to burden the organizers with special flights. So our itinerary was elaborate. We were to land in Allahabad on 13 March and spend the night there. The next day we were to reach Jaunpur, about 120 kilometres away. After the event we were supposed to travel to the holy city of Varanasi, 70 kilometres away from Jaunpur. From Varanasi we were to fly back to Delhi. Travelling through eastern Uttar Pradesh for 200 kilometres in a 4 tonne, bulletproof, airtight, rumbling Ambassador can be extremely exhausting but Dr Kalam always approached difficulties with the unflinching enthusiasm of a twenty-year-old.

We landed at the Allahabad airport late in the afternoon. Our travel entourage was quite large, in accordance with security protocol. The convoy consisted of more than half a dozen vehicles, including an ambulance. Dr Kalam always ensured that I was sitting next to him in his car. Next to the driver sat a Private Security Officer (PSO). His job was to accompany Dr Kalam every single minute. The person always standing behind a VIP, often wearing dark glasses— even when the latter is speaking on stage—is the PSO.

Dr Kalam would often engage in conversation with his PSOs, asking them about the local news and people. In fact, he would always begin his speeches with two sentences spoken in the local language. More often than not, he would learn these local words from his PSOs. While travelling to Jaunpur, Dr Kalam asked the PSO what the area was famous for, but the answer he received shocked us both.

'Sahib, the only thing famous here are the people,' said the PSO.

Even more intrigued, Dr Kalam asked, 'What *kind* of people?'

'*Gundas*,' he said. 'Sahib, we are renowned for housing big gundas. Every household seems to produce at least one gunda. The situation is pathetic.'

Dr Kalam looked at me.

I too am from Uttar Pradesh so I felt compelled to defend this allegation against my home state. 'No, no. It is not so,' I interjected, trying to come up with a few illustrious names to dispel this notion. 'This is the land where Indira Gandhi and Amitabh Bachchan were born!'

But our PSO was more pessimistic than I thought. '*Yeh sab purani baatein hain. Ab to sab mahan gundey hain. Badi moocchon wale gundey.*' (These are all tales of older times. Now we just have infamous goons, goons with thick moustaches.)

I gave up.

The driver, who incidentally donned a bushy moustache himself, shot the PSO an irritated look.

Dr Kalam smiled at my defensive stance. Then he said, 'There is no gunda here! You keep watching. Something good will happen.'

We reached the circuit house in Allahabad late in the evening. As the sun slipped behind the horizon, the weather began to cool down. Soon we were shown into our rooms. It was an old colonial building, a beautiful structure with whitewashed walls and thick, creaky two-panelled doors.

Before dinner, I decided to take a walk around the circuit house. Evening had fallen, bringing with it a swarm of pesky mosquitoes. Sometime during my walk, I heard voices; two men in white clothing were talking to the security personnel at the main gate. A surge of curiosity overwhelmed me, and I decided to find out what was going on.

The men looked like they were from the village. One of them was more than sixty years old, wearing an oversized shirt and trousers with a small cloth towel around his neck. The other was around forty, and he wore a khadi kurta with large mud stains in the front. Both of them were carrying a large dark-coloured sack. I went up to them.

The men were sweating—they had probably travelled some distance on foot. '*Baba, kya hua?*' (Baba, what happened?) I asked.

The younger man spoke Hindi, interspersed with Bhojpuri. 'Sir,' he said, 'we have something special to show to the Jan Rashtrapatiji. We have travelled 40 kilometres just for this.' He lowered the sack and started pulling out a wooden block from it.

Jan Rashtrapati means the People's President, which Dr Kalam was still known as, even after he had left the office of President. It was remarkable to see the resident of a remote village in eastern Uttar Pradesh warmly addressing him by this title.

He continued, 'Sir, this man is my father. I am his eldest son. We have an invention which can change India!'

'What is it? What does it do?' I asked, curious.

'Sir, as inventors of this model, our only condition is that we will reveal it to the Jan Rashtrapatiji. As he is also a scientist, he will surely appreciate it.' The older gentleman could not hide his excitement anymore and interjected, 'This will be very useful for the railways, I am sure!'

I checked my watch; dinner was to be served in ten minutes. Yet I knew that Dr Kalam would not like to miss an opportunity to see the innovations of common citizens.

I recalled his words—'Sometimes the biggest roadblock for the greatest inventor is not the absence of ideas but the lack of opportunity.'

'Come with me,' I said.

The iron gate creaked open. The younger man clutched the sack carefully, indicating that the invention inside was truly precious to him. I ushered them towards Dr Kalam's room where a few policemen were waiting. As soon as we reached, Dr Kalam's door opened. The coincidence caught the father-son duo completely off guard.

10, Rajaji Marg, New Delhi was Dr Kalam's official residence from 2007 to 2015. The ground floor served as his office and a small room on the first floor was his bedroom. The three large windows on the first floor (left) were part of the library and reading room.

Winter, 2012. Dr Kalam posing in his garden on a cold evening. The Arjuna tree is in the background with the setting sun peeking through its leaves.

November 2014. Dr Kalam looking thoughtfully at the Great Wall of China. He was greatly moved by this wonder of the world. According to him it shows that great will is the difference between the impossible and the achievable.

January 2015. Loni, Maharashtra. Dr Kalam posing with the children of a dance troupe. Their performance was called off due to paucity of time but Dr Kalam made it a point to call them to his guest house and spend time with them.

November 2010. A group of rural schoolchildren wrote to Dr Kalam about their newspaper publication called *Bacchon ki Pahel*. Dr Kalam not only met them but also arranged a lecture for them at the Raj Bhavan in Bhopal. We wrote about these children in our first book together—*Target 3 Billion*.

April 2010. Dr Kalam posing with dogwood trees, which he renamed April Bloomers. He is beckoning some children to join him for the photo.

March 2012. The Sujanganj Pranavam Intermediate Rural School in Jaunpur. Great teachers are also humble learners. Dr Kalam decided to become a student; he sat at a desk and asked me to teach him something new. Also in the frame is the principal of the school.

Diwali, 2011. My teacher and I in the garden at 10, Rajaji Marg. All festivals began with him blessing his associates.

June 2002. Dr Kalam filing a nomination form for the post of the President of India. Notice the presence of leaders from almost all political parties around him. In 2012, in the heat of the presidential race, looking at this picture, he reflected, 'I want to see them come together like this, and not make them fight.' Shortly afterwards, he withdrew from the contest

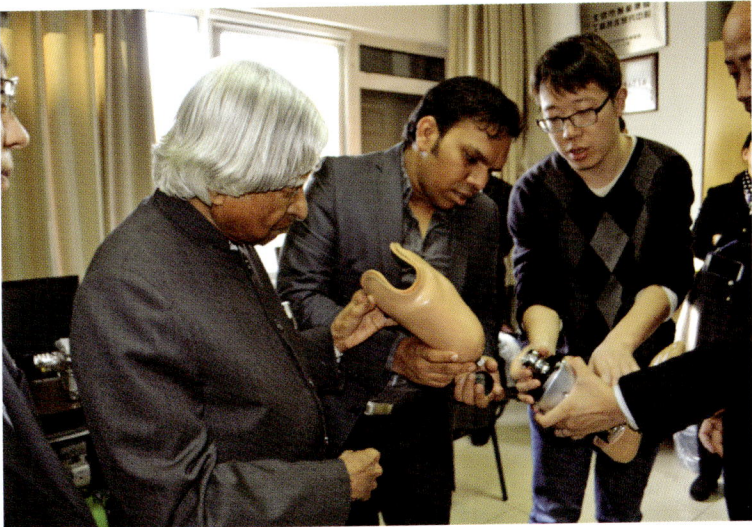

(Above) May 2014. University of Edinburgh. Dr Kalam testing a human-movement-replicating robotic arm.
(Below) November 2014. Peking University. Dr Kalam observing a prosthetic robotic limb for amputees. He always had an eye out for technology that could ease human suffering and help the needy. To him, that was the purpose of science.

April 2010. Dr Kalam and I at the University of Kentucky. The students across the table are presenting their ideas on how social enterprises can solve global problems.

May 2014. Edinburgh Castle. Dr Kalam was particularly interested in the ancient castle visible from his room at the Waldorf Astoria. After much hesitation he agreed to visit it—and we had a wonderful time listening to its 2000-year-old history.

February 2010. Warana in Kolhapur, Maharashtra. Dr Kalam saw this group of sugar-cane farmers outside a sugar mill and instantly got out of his car and went to them. He spoke to the farmers and posed for pictures with them. He always said, 'These are my people.'

March 2012. Allahabad. An elderly ex-railway attendant and his son came to meet Dr Kalam at the circuit house. They showed him their design for a new interlocking system for railway tracks which could stop the *khat-khat* of the rolling wheels. Dr Kalam was highly impressed with the duo.

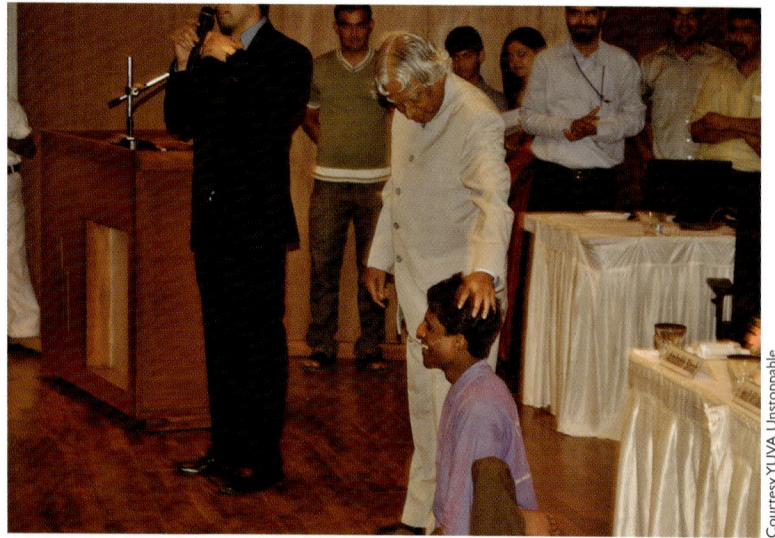

October 2010. Dr Kalam sharing the stage with Raghu, twenty-six, at the five-year celebration of the NGO YUVA Unstoppable in Ahmedabad. This was the only time Dr Kalam met Raghu, an energetic youth who could not stand without support but was always available to help anyone in need. Dr Kalam always remembered Raghu's spirit and his work. When Raghu passed away in an accident in 2013, Dr Kalam wrote an official letter to his family to express his grief.

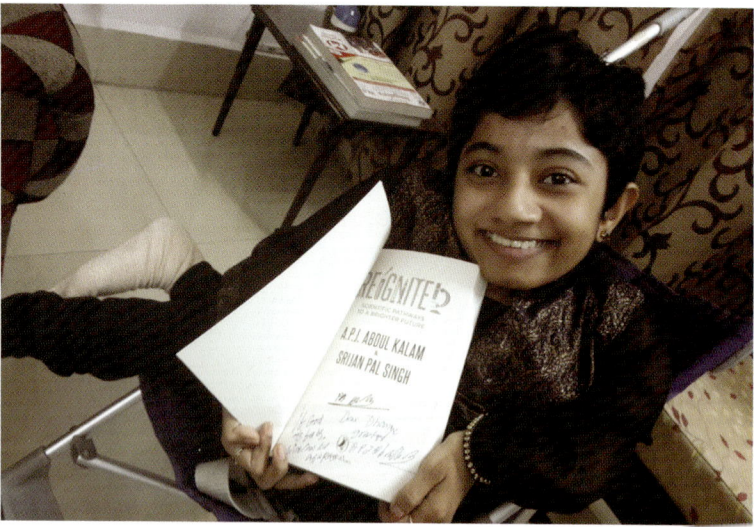

June 2015. Young Dhanya came to meet Dr Kalam in Bengaluru. She has acute brittle-bone disease and has suffered more than 200 fractures. She cannot walk but leads a mission to help others like her. Dr Kalam gifted her our book *Reignited*, which she proudly holds here.

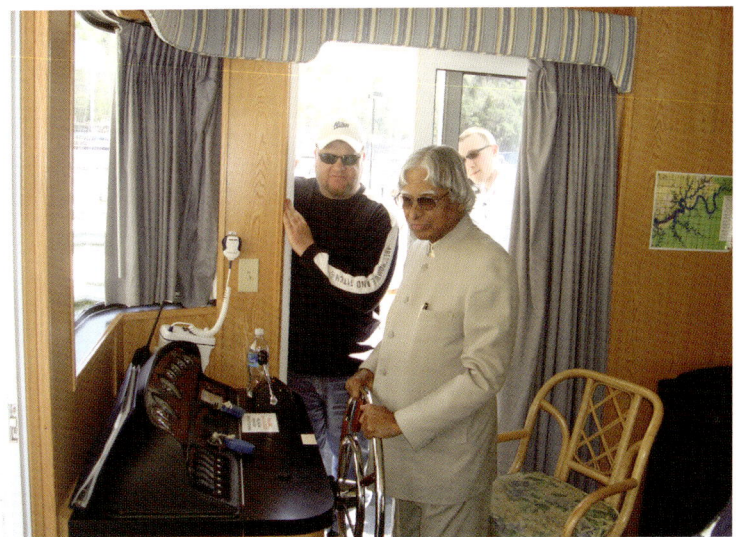

2010. Lake Cumberland, USA. Dr Kalam trying to steer a boat. This was a rare two-hour leisure trip he had agreed to. He usually rejected ideas that required him to take time off from his work, saying, 'I am here to work. Let's work.' On this trip too, he spent his time trying to understand the boat's design and where the man-made lake got its water supply from.

April 2010. Dr Kalam with several civil engineers at the construction site of the healthcare centre being built for the University of Kentucky—a 2-billion-dollar hospital for children. He was impressed by the design of the building, which would create an ambience of healing. He recommended similar designs for healthcare centres across the world.

August 2012. Raj Bhavan, Kolkata. Standing in front of one of the oldest elevators in Asia.

2012. Azamgarh, Uttar Pradesh. Dr Kalam made a sudden stop on the highway at a local tea stall for chai and samosa. He made such unplanned stops quite frequently. He also used the opportunity to learn more about the small local vendors, and shared what he learnt in many of his classes and books.

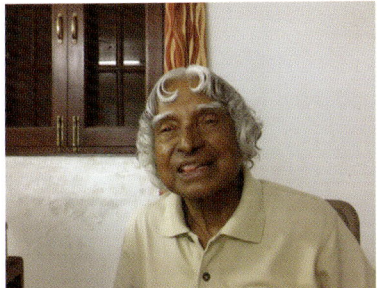

23–24 July 2015. Dr Kalam decided to honour the request of some of Professor Balakrishnan's IISc students—they wanted a video recording from Dr Kalam for their retiring teacher. Dr Kalam and I completed this assignment post midnight, using a stack of books as a tripod and a mobile phone as a camera. Before we started the video recording we decided to try some poses to adjust the angle. These are the last pictures taken of Dr Kalam at his residence in Delhi.

January 2012. Dr Kalam and I in the meeting room on the ground floor at 10, Rajaji Marg.

28 July 2015. Early morning. Raj bhavan, Shillong. This simple dressing table was set up for Dr Kalam in his room. As fate would have it, he never did arrive in this room.

28 July 2015. Early morning. This is a picture of the dining table laid out for Dr Kalam and us. His favourite mango pickle was kept especially for him. Pickle and curd were an integral part of all his meals.

June 2016. The inauguration of the twentieth Kalam Library, in Bangalore. Several such libraries are already in operation across rural India and urban slums.

27 July 2015. IIM Shillong. This is the last picture of Dr Kalam, with the soldier who stood for three hours in the gypsy leading our car as we drove from Guwahati to Shillong. Dr Kalam thanked him for his effort and offered him tea. His final moments were spent with a soldier, and then with the students at IIM Shillong.

Seeing him, the two immediately folded their hands and bowed to him. Their elbows collided as they hurried to touch Dr Kalam's feet.

As I quickly narrated their story to Dr Kalam, he smiled. He seemed to be in no rush for dinner. Seeing their nervousness, he said in Hindi, 'Dikhaiye! Kya hai?' (Show us! What is it?)

The old man found courage in these words. He pulled out two large, wooden blocks, with wedges at their ends, from the sack. The items seemed custom-made. He fitted the pieces perfectly together and then pulled them apart again. He then fitted them back together and began to tell his story.

'Sahib! I am not very educated. I failed class six twice, so my father forced me to take up simple jobs. Thankfully I got a job in the Indian Railways. In fact, I have worked in the railways for most of my life. I have travelled as an attendant in the Northern Railways, journeying many thousands of miles in my career. I just loved boarding trains and going to distant places. But I experienced one problem. Whenever I tried to sleep, I was disturbed by the khat-khat, khat-khat sound of the carriage wheels rolling over the railway tracks. I noticed that my passengers didn't like the racket either. Even the ones in the AC compartments were bothered by it.'

I could see that they had got Dr Kalam's attention.

The old man's son, who was standing nearby, took the wooden block from his father and continued playing with the two pieces, pulling them apart and assembling them back again. He seemed thrilled to be able to show Dr Kalam their invention.

The old father continued his story. 'I did not understand why the train made this sound. So I went about asking everyone. I asked the teacher at school, the elderly people in villages, and the officers in the railways, but nobody ever gave me an answer.'

He wiped his face with towel on his shoulders and continued with renewed vigour.

'Rashtrapati Sahib, I am a small man. But I wanted to solve this problem of the masses. Crores of people travel in the railways every day, and I wanted to bring ease to them. Then one day, a young engineer, who was travelling in the train, struck up a conversation with me. He told me that the gaps which are left in the railway tracks are the reason for the sound. I stared at the railway tracks and indeed noticed the gaps, which were left there in order to accommodate the expansion and compression of metallic rivets.' His voice had gained confidence by now, and Dr Kalam and the others around him were listening to him with rapt attention.

He then took the wooden blocks from his son and displayed it proudly. 'I went home and every night I started working on wooden planks, trying to make a better track-joint so that there won't be any more of that noise when the train runs. I am also a part-time carpenter, you see. Everybody laughed at me, saying that I was poor and uneducated and that I wouldn't be able to do any of this. I should rather do manual labour is what they said.'

He looked at Dr Kalam, as if trying to read something on his face, before continuing.

'Then *you* became the President. I was so inspired by your story. I told all those villagers that if one poor man can make missiles fly, then another poor man can make the trains run smoother. So I tried and tried, for four or five years, and finally came up with this design.' He pointed at the joint between the two wooden wedges. 'This is an interlocking device and, yet, it provides room for expansion as well. I am sure this will end the *khat-khat* forever.' He folded his hands and, seeing him, his son did the same.

'Sahib, I don't need any money for this. I just came here to ensure that this reaches the right people, so that they can actually implement it. I am sure this will help the nation at large. People can sleep well, even on wheels!' Saying this, he handed the model to me.

I hesitated.

Dr Kalam was greatly moved. The innovation and benevolence of the old man had clearly struck him. He said to him, '*Bohot achha!*' (Very good!) And then he asked me to translate the next few sentences.

'I am very glad to see your sensitivity and your innovation. You have a very kind mind to have thought of solving the problems of so many. I will take photos of your model and send them to the railway people and share them with everyone on the Internet. You are a fellow scientist, dear friend!'

Then he paused, turning around to the pessimistic PSO.

'*Dekhiye!* See, what Allahabad is producing. *These* are the people we need to remember.'

The PSO nodded sheepishly in agreement.

I took photos of the model on my phone, and Dr Kalam happily posed with it. It was almost 9 p.m. by then. The old innovator and his son were brimming with happiness and hope as they put the model back inside their sack.

Dr Kalam then whispered to me, 'Get them some fruits before they leave.'

I went inside his room, where a bowl of fruits was kept on the table. I picked up a handful and returned. Dr Kalam handed them the fruits and said, 'This is for your journey back. I know it must be tiring. Scientists should eat well.'

The men shook hands with Dr Kalam and bowed again in respect. The old man scribbled down his name and number on a piece of paper. His name was Ram Avatar.

Later, after dinner, as per our usual practice, we went for a stroll outside the main compound.

'The man whom we met a while ago? He is a true scientist at heart. He had four key things,' Dr Kalam said. 'He was a keen observer. He was sensitive to the problems of others.

He was a persistent learner. And finally, he did not give up even in the face of poverty. He was poor in income but rich in ideas. True richness comes from innovative thinking, a sensitive heart and a smiling face—money is just a fleeting thing. I am fortunate to have met him.'

'And as for our dear PSO, I hope he has learnt that he needs to let up on his pessimism, and not on Allahabad,' I added.

We both smiled and headed back to our respective rooms.

Two days later, the information about the model was sent to the railway officials. Ram Avatar and his son were featured on Dr Kalam's social media page, along with their model.

Soon after, Dr Kalam called me to his office. 'I have a story for you,' he said.

As I entered the library and sat down, he said, 'Remember that guy who met us with that model of the railway track?'

I nodded.

He smiled and said, 'People better take him seriously. I am going to tell you a story about something similar.'

So the story began.

'In the late seventeenth century, Britain established the Royal Observatory. The aim of this observatory was to improve navigation at sea. One of the biggest problems in those days was that the sailors could not predict the longitudes accurately. Hence they were not exactly sure of their location. Back then there was no GPS!'

'Of course,' I said.

He continued, 'You see, Britain ruled the world largely because of its superior naval powers and so the Royal Observatory had the critical task of solving the problem of inaccurate longitudes. Back then, Britain had the best scientists and astronomers. Thus the Royal Observatory called on the great Isaac Newton and even the comet expert, Edmond Halley. But even the greatest minds could not solve this problem then.

'Things became really bad in the early 1700s. Sir Shovell paid heavily when he miscalculated the longitude and four ships were wrecked due to thick fog near Italy. More people died in the accident than aboard the *Titanic*. The Royal Observatory, under tremendous pressure to solve the longitude problem, tried a new method.

'Instead of relying on a handful of known experts it decided to approach the public with the challenge. A huge amount, £20,000 (about £3 million in today's value), was declared as reward for anyone who could solve the challenge. Naturally, they expected some astronomer to solve this— after all, this issue was about the science of spotting and understanding the stars.

'But the solution came from an unexpected source. A self-educated carpenter called John Harrison offered one with almost no application of astronomy. He designed a clock which worked so accurately at sea that by measuring the sun the exact longitude could be calculated. A problem which even Newton could not solve was eventually solved by a simple carpenter. Such is life. Such is science. Such is progress.'

He lay back and relaxed in his chair.

'So I say that we should take our carpenter friend seriously,' he reiterated.

'He may indeed silence the *khat-khat*,' I said.

I got up and left, closing the door on my way out, which shut behind me with a creak. It could do with a carpenter too.

Oath for Villagers

Dr Kalam had great hopes from rural India, and he would often visit the hinterland of the nation—the schools, hospitals, administration and private CSR functions in remote villages. Whenever we interacted with rural citizens he would administer a special oath to them. When we went to Hindi-speaking villages, he would ask me to translate the oath as he spoke.

- Children are as precious as wealth.
- We will give equal importance to male and female children in the society. They will have

equal claim to education and rights to facilitate equality in their growth.

- We will raise a small family, for the health and prosperity of the society at large.
- Our income is earned by hard work. We will not waste it by gambling and drinking.
- We need to tell our children about the importance of education, as learning imparts knowledge, which paves the way to success.
- We need to come together to protect our forests and prevent pollution.
- We will plant at least five saplings.
- We will become role models for our children.

19

Freedom Chai

In 2012, we visited Pune to attend a few functions that were being held across various schools and colleges. Pune's commercial airport is shared with the Indian Air Force, hence the number of flights going in and out of the city is restricted to certain 'open' hours when the military does not use the airbase. We arrived in the city the evening before the scheduled events.

We stayed at the newly renovated government guest house—a beautiful white building with a large dome. At night, we proceeded for our usual post-dinner walk. This was a cell-phone-free time, and we would have candid conversations about almost everything under the sun. We walked through a flower-lined path that ran along the perimeter of the garden. Under protocol, two guards followed us, mapping every moment and every turn we made. Dr Kalam said to the trailing guards, 'You can go home. Or you can sit down and keep watch. *Aap baithiye!*' (You sit!)

The guards didn't sit. Instead, they slowed down and fell back, maintaining enough space between us so that we could continue our conversation in private.

Soon we approached the main gate—a large iron structure which had been left ajar. We had a full view of the city outside. There was the usual bustle of the market and the traffic, and people scurrying about everywhere. We stopped to enjoy the view; it captured Dr Kalam's attention much more than it did mine. For me it was a common scene, but for him it was almost a novelty.

Just then a bus roared past us. A thought struck me. 'When was the last time you took a bus?' I asked him.

He looked at me and said, 'At least seventeen to eighteen years ago, when I was working on a project in Odisha, perhaps near Chandipur.'

I saw some heaviness in his reply.

'I wonder when was the last time you went out without security guards following you?' I asked.

'Sometime in the mid-90s. It was long, long ago. I remember I used to travel on highways and we would often stop by local dhabas. There was this dhaba on a highway in Odisha which sold hot milk that was thickened by bringing it to a boil. And the guy there would give us a glass full of that milk straight from the pan. Just one glass of that, and you were set for the day.'

Hot milk remained a part of his diet till the end. Every night post dinner, Dr Kalam would drink one full glass.

He continued, now reflecting and ruing. 'Sometimes, I feel like I'm in a jail—like one where people cannot move outside their cell. That is exactly how my life is. The only difference is that my cell is bigger and the food is better, but my freedom is curtailed. Not even the weakest of birds are happy in the shiniest of cages. Freedom to move about is precious, I tell you.

'Enjoy while you have it. I miss the dhabas. Make sure you cherish the little joys of life while they last. Maybe someday you will be surrounded by security too.'

As we turned back towards the guest house, I saw him cast a longing glance at the half-open gate. The guards had started to close it. Perhaps it was a security hazard to keep it ajar.

* * *

The idea that a VVIP's life was similar to that of a prisoner's stayed with me.

On the flight back to Delhi, I suddenly had an idea. I turned to Dr Kalam and said, 'Why don't I get my car one day and we can sneak you out of your house. We will visit India Gate and come back quickly. It will hardly take fifteen minutes and we can use the back gate to let ourselves out.'

As I had expected, he laughed. 'You see, there are so many security people who work at home. They will all get into trouble if I do this.'

I knew my idea was bound to be struck down. But the thought of visiting India Gate freely did bring a smile to his face.

Weeks later, we went to eastern Uttar Pradesh as we had to visit Allahabad, Varanasi and Azamgarh. One of the events that we were scheduled to attend was organized by the district administration; they had brought children from many government schools of Azamgarh. Once again we arrived in Allahabad. We landed in the evening before the event and planned to depart from Varanasi the next day, after the function.

The next morning, although we had set out from the Allahabad guest house on time, we encountered some roadblocks and that slowed us down considerably.

To our disappointment, we reached the gathering half an hour late, but the organizers were kind enough to adjust the programme schedule so that the children did not have to wait. We Indians are perhaps the best at managing unsuspected delays and occurrences. As a friend from the West once told us, 'Indians know best how to ride the horse of chaos.'

The same day we had to visit another spot. Our flight back to Delhi was scheduled from Varanasi and, on the way, we had to attend another short function at a hospital in Azamgarh, called the Vedanta Hospital. Azamgarh is the birth city of the famous Urdu poet Kaifi Azmi. After wrapping up the function we set out towards Varanasi for our flight back.

All along the highway we noticed a number of small shops huddled together—some were selling tea and snacks, a few paan shops were selling Benarasi paan, and some others were selling clothes and electronics. There were some high-end restaurants too, declaring 'Air Conditioned' or 'Air Cooled' in thick fonts, and, of course, there were several pharmaceutical shops. Any rural or semi-urban road in India is lined with shops like these. Such a diverse blend and balance of commodities represents the 'horizontal supermarkets', where one can find almost anything they need. In these markets, there are no designated corridors or floors, or even a shop layout—the entire planning is organic, market-driven and innovation-scaled.

As expected, I could see my guru fascinated by these rural commercial spaces. He was looking longingly at the many dhabas that we were whizzing past. That is when I remembered his Odisha story. I decided to give my idea another try. 'Sir, why don't you relive the Odisha dhaba experience here? We can surely ask the convoy to make a quick stop. We will grab a chai and leave in five minutes.'

I expected him to decline, but to my surprise, he asked curiously, 'Can we do this?' His voice had a spark of anticipation in it.

'Of course,' I replied, though I was not sure how to actually pull it off.

So I turned to our driver and our PSO and asked them if they could connect wirelessly to the pilot vehicle—the first car in the convoy—and make a stop at the next dhaba. The POS looked surprised and said, '*Sahib ko chai lena hai, badhiya hotel chalein. Yahan se paanch kos door ek bada hotel hai—*' (Sir wants to have tea so we should go to a fancy hotel. There is a big hotel five kilometres ahead—)

Before he could complete his suggestion, Dr Kalam interjected, 'Not *bada* hotel. We will go to a dhaba.'

The security personnel seemed amused and the driver tried his best to suppress a smile.

The wireless message was sent out to the pilot car and, in a few minutes, it stopped at a small dhaba called the Sai Chai Shop, named after the famous saint who was born in Shirdi, Maharashtra.

At the shop, the shopkeeper sat behind a large glass counter. A vast array of Indian dishes was displayed in the glass cabinet, ranging from samosas and pakoras to jalebis and burfis. Beside the counter was a refrigerator, stacked with branded colas and our famous local drink, *banta*.[1] Seeing our large convoy and the many policemen, the shopkeeper hurried out from behind the counter and placed a few plastic chairs around a small table. He said his name was Kuber, named after the divine custodian of wealth in Hindu mythology.

'What is today's special dish?' we asked him.

Kuber replied with an air of confidence, 'Everything here is fresh, and restocked twice a day.' He added, 'I am a specialist in flavoured masala chai!'

---

[1] Carbonated water with a dash of lime juice, rock salt and sugar added to it.

Encouraged, we asked him what he meant by 'specialist' in tea. He handed us a laminated menu. The sheet had at least a dozen different flavours of tea—everything from ginger, lemon, chocolate and mint to cardamom, Darjeeling and many others. It was surprising to see such a little shop on an obscure highway doing business with such imagination and vigour. Time for us was limited so we quickly ordered about a dozen cups of tea for all of us, along with some samosas. Kuber and his helper got to work immediately and, five minutes later, we were handed steaming cups and snacks.

We had ordered a special cardamom tea, which had a very refreshing flavour. So we gave it a new name—Freedom Chai or the tea of freedom.

* * *

Soon our Freedom Chai stops became more regular. But these stops gave us more than just freedom; they taught us three unique lessons about India.

First, it showed us how local markets can produce successful entrepreneurs. India is filled with consumers whose purchasing power is average. A small market, even in remote areas like Azamgarh, has enough 'GDP' to support these entrepreneurs.

Second, these small entrepreneurs showcase innovation. Kuber had told us how he had spent many days studying different varieties of tea, and had customized them according to the local flavours. He had gone all the way to the district headquarters to get his menu altered and reprinted many times.

Third, enterprises can be built in a local context. While there is nothing wrong with large, global food chains—they have their own value—these entrepreneurs can also find their niche spaces among the customers in local areas. It is a delicate balance of demand-production-supply, which needs to be handled carefully. Kuber's fridge, stocked with both the local banta and international cola, was a testimony to how domestic and regional brands can coexist with global brands.

These ideas made us seriously think about India's local economic power. And three years later, our thoughts took the shape of Dr Kalam's final book, *Advantage India*.

I Will Fly

The thirteenth-century Persian poet Jalaluddin Muhammad Rumi was one of Dr Kalam's favourites. He would often quote the following verses by Rumi to the youngsters he met—

What Can I Give?

Wings to Fly

I am born with potential.
I am born with goodness and trust.
I am born with ideas and dreams.
I am born with greatness.
I am born with confidence.
I am born with wings.
So, I am not meant for crawling,
I have wings, I will fly
I will fly and fly.

20

Why Did You Not Get Married?

There was one cheeky question that would occasionally crop up in conversations with Dr Kalam, and he would always avoid it with some hilarious tangential anecdote, which usually left people in splits. The question was why he never got married.

In 2011, during a function in Mumbai, a relatively senior member of the audience asked the same question but in a circuitous way, 'Sir, I am sixty years old. You can see I have lost almost all my hair. In fact, most people my age—or even those younger than me—are bald. You are at least twenty years older than me, but your hair is still like that of a rockstar! Do you think the fact that you are a bachelor has something to do with this?' He paused and then pushed further, 'And why are you a bachelor?'

The audience burst into laughter. Even Dr Kalam, who was onstage, could not stop laughing at this for a good half-minute. As the laughter died down, he replied, 'Well, I am a scientist and I can tell you that there is no scientific evidence to suggest this correlation.'

Once again, the hall burst into laughter and in that commotion he avoided the second part of the question.

The day passed and we returned to Raj Bhavan, situated in the Malabar Hills. It is a magnificent building sprawling along the Arabian Sea. We walked around the little garden, watching the huge waves rise and crash on the shore. The question had been bothering me the whole time, and I couldn't help but ask him, 'So, sir, you did not fully answer a question today . . .'

'Which one?'

'There was this person who wanted to know why you're a bachelor. You told him some funny story but you did not answer!'

'You are a funny fellow, I say,' he replied. 'There were a dozen fellows of my age, and even older, in my house, when I was young. They all got married. I was the youngest among them. If one fellow did not get married then what is the difference?'

He was in a particularly light mood so I decided to keep probing. 'But you still didn't answer his question well enough.'

'What *was* the question?' he asked.

'Why are you a bachelor?'

'That question is incomplete.'

I knew I was making him uneasy, but he was still taking it in good humour so I continued. 'Oh, now you will find faults with the question. That's not fair!' I complained.

'I am telling you, I'll give only 50 per cent marks for that question. He asked me about being a bachelor. I am not just a bachelor, I am a *brahmachari!*'

We came to an intersection, and he quickly turned to his right. I was biting my tongue, trying to stop myself from giggling.

'But sir, are the two not the same thing? What is the difference?' I don't know where I found the courage to ask such a bold question. Of course I knew what the difference was between the two.

He suspected that I was pulling his leg but decided to answer it nevertheless, just to get rid of me.

'You don't know? You are funny. There is a difference and now you will figure it out. You see, if you are a brahmachari, you are definitely a bachelor. But if you are a bachelor, you need not be a brahmachari. Got it?'

He did not even wait for me to answer and quickly said, 'Okay, enough. Is dinner ready? Go and check. Go, I say.'

'But it's only 8 p.m. Dinner is at 9—'

'Then go and find out what they are cooking,' he urged impatiently.

I left giggling.

21

If You Cannot Control Fear, Ignore It

On 29 October 2014, Dr Kalam was scheduled to visit the Piramal School in the Bagar district of Rajasthan. The Piramal Foundation for Education Leadership (PFEL), under the leadership of Mr Ajay Piramal, had taken some unique initiatives to promote inclusive education in India. The Piramal School was started as a part of this initiative.

Bagar is difficult to reach. It is about 250 kilometres from Delhi and there is no direct commercial flight connecting Delhi to Bagar. There is a small airstrip in the nearby town of Jhunjhunu, which is forty-five minutes away from Bagar. The people at the Piramal Foundation were kind enough to offer us their private aircraft so we could fly from Delhi to Jhunjhunu. Dr Kalam and I were accompanied by Mr Prasad, who worked in our office, and Mr Harender Sikka, the president of the Piramal Group.

During our conversation, we found out that Mr Sikka had served in the Indian Navy as a naval pilot. He gave us many insights into the pharmaceutical industry. We had a particularly long discussion on the topic of spurious drugs and it was almost a shock to learn that this problem had become rampant. Mr Sikka also told us about some illegal factories where talcum powder was used to fill up capsules. When a person running such an illegal outfit was caught, his defence was, 'But talcum powder is not injurious to health!'

'This is poisoning the faith one has in the medical system,' Dr Kalam said, concerned about the situation.

In less than an hour we landed at Jhunjhunu, where we were received by the district authorities and by Ajay Piramal himself. He was a tall man, well over six feet tall, and he always wore a smile on his face. Dr Kalam, Mr Piramal and I set out together for Bagar in an SUV and during the journey Mr Piramal told us about the famous Piramal Fellowship, about PFEL and about the Piramal School.

We learnt that PFEL worked with headmasters across 787 government schools to create future leaders of the country. This initiative had impacted more than 1 lakh children. The Piramal Fellowship, formerly called the Gandhi Fellowship, is a unique two-year programme in which university graduates and professionals are sent to work in rural areas for a period of two years. The young Piramal Fellows are mainly required to work in tandem with the headmasters of the schools, which are situated in the middle of rural hinterlands. It is important to help the principals because they are responsible for shaping young, impressionable students, and so they can have an impact on how society is shaped as a whole. We headed straight to the Piramal School once we reached Bagar. It was a well-designed campus, covering an area of 44,000 square feet.

At the school we met almost fifty young Piramal Fellows, both men and women, who had come from different parts of India and also from foreign countries. We also met a group of school principals with whom these young Fellows were working and it was heartening to hear them praise the hard work and sincere efforts of these young Fellows. We were shown some educational games which the Fellows had developed along with the principals. One game was particularly impressive; it was an improvised version of the traditional game of snakes and ladders, meant to teach mathematics to children in an interesting way. These young professionals had transformed a medieval game into a tool for education in these rural areas. The Piramal Fellows had an immense impact on us.

Despite Mr Prasad's warnings, we spent much more than the scheduled time at the Piramal School, learning all about the innovative activities that the Fellows were conducting there. Consequently, we were late for the next programme that we were supposed to attend that day in a local school. But we were now adept at managing small delays in Dr Kalam's programme—we would simply adjust the length of his speech and cut down the non-essential and ceremonial part of the event.

While Dr Kalam was speaking at that programme we received a message from the two pilots who were waiting in the Jhunjhunu airstrip for us. We were reminded that we had to reach the airstrip before 5.30 p.m. because it did not have the facilities to operate at night. If we took more time we would not get the clearance to fly, which would mean spending the night in Jhunjhunu.

When we received that message it was already 4.45 p.m. and Dr Kalam was just halfway through his speech.

To understand what happened next you will have to know how Dr Kalam conducted his speeches. A standard computer monitor used to be placed on the lectern. The input wire of this monitor would be connected to my laptop. Both of us could see the same pages on our respective monitors. We called it the 'system'. Anything that I typed on my laptop would show up on Dr Kalam's screen. Using this system, I could send him any relevant data required while answering questions from the audience. Often we would have a bit of fun with our audiences. During important cricket matches I would relay live scores and updates about wicket losses to him. Dr Kalam, being the witty person that he was, would pass the news to the crowds who would then start cheering. And all of this would happen mid-speech. The 'system' was also our real-time translator. Whenever someone asked Dr Kalam a question in the local language I would quickly translate it to English and send it to him. If I didn't understand the language, then the local security officer who would be sitting next to me would help me out. In this way we ensured that Dr Kalam never had to ask anyone to translate the questions. This was how he connected with the audience and showed respect for local languages. Our 'system' was simple and reliable.

Coming back to our transportation worries—the airstrip was at least twenty to twenty-five minutes away from the local school, which meant that we had to leave within the next twenty minutes so we could make the deadline. I desperately needed to stop him from taking questions at the end of his speech. As soon as his speech got over I typed on my laptop—

'Pilots are searching for you everywhere. Planes here don't fly in the darkness. If we don't leave now, they will take off without us and we can have a Rajasthani dinner tonight.'

I had now learnt how to convey serious messages in humorous tones to him. He read the message, turned to smile at me and stepped away from the microphone. Then he asked me, 'Do you want a Rajasthani dinner?'

I typed back, 'Yes. But we'd better take it with us to Delhi. Take only TWO questions. 2=2.'

'2=2' was my usual way of telling him emphatically not to take more than two questions from the audience. But he never entertained such requests from me and usually went on to take at least six!

He turned to the crowd again and announced, 'My computer says that you should take only two questions, or else your flight will leave without you. So two fellows run up to the stage and ask.'

He took four questions nevertheless and the event concluded in a rush.

When we finally left, it was 5.10 p.m. I noticed that the previously dry potholes on the roads were now filled with water. In the closed auditorium of the school, we hadn't realized that there had been an unexpected shower outside.

The pilots called again. This time the news was graver. They said that there was a storm coming, which meant that they might not be able to fly at all.

We reached the airstrip in the nick of time. It wasn't raining and the winds were not that strong yet, so the pilots decided to take off quickly. The engines had been left running in anticipation of our arrival, so we were airborne in less than three minutes. We heaved a sigh of relief as soon as we were in the air. Five minutes into the flight, the lights in the six-seater plane went off, and the aircraft started shaking uncontrollably due to the terrible weather. Outside, the sky was pitch black, even though it was just 5.45 p.m. The turbulence became more and more terrifying, and the plane started losing height gradually. It would fall through the air for a few metres and then become steady again. This happened a couple of times. Since Mr Sikka had been a naval officer he tried to calm us down. In small planes like the one we were flying in, there are no gates separating the passenger area from the cockpit. So Mr Sikka asked the pilot what the problem was with the plane from his seat. The pilot looked back at us and shrugged helplessly; he too was clueless about what was happening.

When a pilot says he doesn't know what the problem is, it is like a doctor telling you he is not sure of what is happening in the middle of a surgery. Suddenly all of us were alarmed. Every human being has a different way of combating fear, and no matter how good we are at acting, when death stares us in the face we react to it with our own unique primitive responses. I went silent, holding on to the glass of water kept in front of me to prevent it from falling every time the plane dived into darkness. Mr Prasad, who was sitting on my left, leaned against the window and closed his eyes; beads of perspiration dotted his forehead. Mr Sikka began to pray. Dr Kalam, who was sitting across me, tried to smile but soon he too lost his nerve. The tiny craft was filled with the loud sound of rain battering it from all sides. I was convinced that the wings would break off any moment now, but I couldn't stop myself from looking out into the storm through the plane window.

Suddenly I saw the window shut. I realized that it was Dr Kalam who had shut it.

Before I could say anything, he said, 'When you can't control the variables, learn to ignore the consequences. If you don't look at the fears which are beyond your control, you will find it easier to counter them.'

To be honest, at that moment I was too terrified to understand the profundity of that statement. I was convinced that we were going to crash, and my mind was filled with horrifying images.

The ordeal continued for another fifteen minutes and then suddenly the pilot yelled, 'Light!'

We turned to look out through the cockpit. Through the windscreen we could see a circle of blue light. As we flew towards it, the circle kept growing bigger in size. Soon we zipped into it and the sky turned bright around us once again. The rain had stopped too.

When the pilot announced that we were going to land in Delhi soon, we cheered in relief.

Later that evening I had to take another flight to Ahmedabad. I stayed back at the airport while the others left. My flight was delayed by two hours. When I finally boarded the flight, the pilot explained the reason for the delay—a sudden storm had struck somewhere near Delhi and so all the flights had been cancelled for one hour that evening. I realized that we had been caught in that same storm.

When I landed in Ahmedabad, I got a call from Dr Kalam. He asked me if I was fine. Then we got drawn into a conversation about the storm that we had been caught in earlier that day.

'I too had thought that we would end up in a crash,' he said.

We laughed at the danger that we had been in not very long ago. I then asked him, 'You told me to combat uncontrollable fears by ignoring them. I guess it worked well for me. But what did you do to combat *your* fear?'

'I was trying to help you guys forget your fears. That way I was ignoring my own.'

Three days later when I was back in Delhi, I wrote him a little note:

Dr Kalam's Two Laws of Fear:

1. To manage uncontrollable fear, try to ignore it.
2. If the first law doesn't work for you, try to focus on helping others to apply the first law. You can conquer your fear by diverting your attention to others.

He took the note, and said, 'I will remember them. We will write about them someday. Add one more to it.

'Fear breeds fear, courage breeds courage.'

'Indeed. The three laws are now complete,' I said.

22

My Only Regret

In 2014, we visited Mumbai to attend the 50th anniversary celebrations of a local college. It was a modest celebration, and Dr Kalam was happy to see that the college was catering to students from low-income families, giving them quality education at affordable fees.

Just before attending this function we had been to another grand event that was organized by a corporate firm. When the college principal found out about the event that we were coming from, he was slightly embarrassed because his event was just a small and modest affair in comparison. As we made our way to the seminar hall, the principal said to us apologetically, 'Sir, we have very limited means and resources, so we could not organize a big event. Please pardon us. But the next time we will make sure we give you a bigger welcome.'

'Will you do something if I ask you to?' Dr Kalam enquired as he continued towards the hall.

The principal could only nod in agreement.

'You collect as many resources as you can for the next time I come.'

I turned to look at him, surprised. This was completely unlike him.

'And when you have collected all of it, do not waste the money on putting up posters of me. I think these people would know me even without posters. Rather, use the money to help the economically weaker students in your college. You should institute even better scholarships—that should be your goal. That will be the best way to organize this function. You are anyway doing a great job of running this college, just keep up the good work of making it affordable for students. Okay?'

The principal agreed. He looked proud at that moment. This was the magic of Dr Kalam. He always highlighted the dignity and honour of another person's work. This was the quality of a great leader—a great leader can enable others to discover their own self-worth.

Dr Kalam was greeted with a lot of cheering when he entered the hall. Through his speech he addressed the concerns of the youth who had come from challenging economic conditions. He spoke about his own life, his failures and his successes. He spoke of the great Nobel Laureate Mario Capecchi, a victim of the Second World War, who had lost most of his family in the war. He had to spend his childhood in an orphanage. But despite his difficulties, he persevered and went on to discover DNA, which won him the greatest prize in science in the world.

At the end of his speech, Dr Kalam was given a standing ovation. This was followed by a question-and-answer session. Dr Kalam answered each question with his usual wit and grace.

Suddenly, a young student of about twenty stood up to ask a question. He was standing at the back of the hall and the mic did not reach him in time so he shouted out his question, 'Dr Kalam, you have had so many successes. I am sure you had some failures too. You always say that you have built your successes over the lessons learnt from failures. I want to know something. Is there something that you could not do, and still regret not doing it?'

Interesting question, I thought.

It was the first time someone had asked him this question and our entire team was curious to hear his response.

Dr Kalam took his time to think through the answer and finally replied, 'You know, back home, I have an elder brother who is ninety-eight years old now. He can walk slowly, but steadily, and completely on his own. He has a little problem with his vision and hence there is always a need to keep the house well lit, especially in the night.

'Now you see, in Rameswaram, there are power cuts sometimes. Thus it becomes difficult for him to move about freely. So, last year I got a rooftop solar panel installed at home, with a good battery. When the sun shines, the panel gives power, and in the night the battery takes over the power supply. Now there is plenty of power all the time. My brother is happy.

'When I see him happy, I also feel happy. But I am also reminded of my own parents. Both of them lived for almost a hundred years and towards their later years they had difficulty seeing things well. Three decades ago, the power cuts were more frequent. Back then I could do nothing for them. There was no solar power. The fact that I could not do anything to remove their pain is my greatest regret, something which will remain with me forever.'

The answer touched a chord in the hearts of everyone in the audience. Here was a person, more than eighty years old, who had achieved so much in life, but still had the compassion and the humility to speak publicly about his greatest failure. He was still bothered about failing his parents. How many of us think of such things?

I couldn't help but wonder when I had last stopped to consider my parents' situation, when I had tried to do anything to ease their burden. In the rat race of life, we often forget about the people who give us everything they have and make us who we are.

23

Centenary Celebrations

Dr Kalam was very close to his elder brother, Janaab A.P.J. Maracayer. He was sixteen years older than Dr Kalam and was like a father figure to him. He had counselled Dr Kalam on several important decisions and was also his spiritual guide. The bond between the two brothers was very strong. In the library, where Dr Kalam used to spend most of his time, there was a photograph of the two brothers. While one brother was in his eighties, the other was nearing a hundred. All the members of Dr Kalam's family had had long lives.

In 2015, in the month of May, Dr Kalam's brother dropped by for a visit. It was a special moment as Janaab A.P.J. Maracayer was about to turn ninety-nine in a few months. His birthday was on the 5th of November. The day his brother was leaving for Rameswaram, Dr Kalam met him over dinner. He said to me later, 'You fellow, listen. My brother will turn ninety-nine years old in November. Tell me, now by the end of this year, how many orbits will he have completed around the sun?'

This was the question he always asked on people's birthdays. A true rocket engineer, he loved equating years to the number of orbits the earth had made around the sun and the number of orbits the moon had made around the earth.

I was familiar with this question by now.

'Hundredth orbit!' I replied.

'Right. Now listen, you fellow. You see, next year, in November 2016, my brother will be a hundred years old. He has never celebrated his birthday in a big way. On his 100th birthday, I want to throw him a big surprise party. He would love it, right?'

'Of course! He would love it,' I reassured him. 'We should do it. Where do you want to celebrate?'

Dr Kalam got really excited. 'I think it should be at his home only—that way he will not see the surprise coming. We can also gather all the family—the grandchildren, the great-grandchildren—everyone. There will be about fifty fellows like that. But I have a problem—I don't know how to go about it. You fellow must know how to organize birthday parties. I will send you to Rameswaram at the beginning of November 2016, and you can help my guys over there to set up a big birthday party. I will go later and join you. It must be a good one for his three-figure age. What do you think?'

'Yes, sure, I will plan out something and present it to you,' I replied.

I'm sure organizing someone's 100th birthday party would be a novelty for most people!

Then he threw me another question.

'And what gift should I give him?'

I was caught off-guard. I didn't have any answer to this. What can you give a 100-year-old person? I wriggled out of it saying, 'Sir, his birthday is still a year away. We will think of something after your birthday in October. What do you say?'

'Okay. We will wait,' he said.

But I could sense that he wasn't happy with the answer. I returned to the office, knowing that I had disappointed him.

I gathered some writing material and went back to the reading room where he was sitting. For the next half an hour, we sat planning the details of the party. We thought of everything, from banners saying '100' to Tamil songs to be played in the party. We came up with many ideas for commemorating the occasion and finally decided to open a hundred libraries across rural India. A hundred libraries for a hundred years on earth. Dr Kalam was very happy with the idea. We decided to begin working on it by July.

As fate would have it, seven weeks after this planning session Dr Kalam passed away. We never got to show him the hundred libraries or the detailed plans for the event.

Dr Kalam never lived to see his brother's 100th revolution around the sun. But then the sun is a star, and it is said that great people become the brightest of stars after their death.

The light from the powerful stars that are burning far away from us at incomprehensible distances takes a long time to reach us, sometimes hundreds of years. But such light does reach us some day, irrespective of the distance. It is believed that these bright stars keep a watch over us. Considering that this belief is true, a small number of us Kalam followers started the Kalam Library Project in December 2015. By the time this book reaches you, we would have perhaps already completed the target of opening a hundred libraries. And by reading this book, you are becoming a part of this project because the proceeds from this book will be used to open more and more such libraries.

Just as Dr Kalam desired.

24

I Learnt a Life Lesson in Giving

On 5 June 2014, Dr Kalam, Dhanshyam Sharma (his personal assistant) and I visited the Indian Institute of Technology (IIT), Indore for their convocation ceremony.

IIT Indore is one of the newest additions in the prestigious network of IITs across India. In fact, this was only its second convocation ceremony. Dr Kalam, an institution-builder himself, had an affinity for fledgling campuses. To help and encourage them to grow, he often visited these new institutions. Some such institutions that he was attached to were the IITs in Patna, Hyderabad and Indore, the Indian Institute of Information Technology (IIIT), Hyderabad, the Indian Institute of Space Sciences and Technology (IIST), Kerala where he was the chancellor, and, of course, IIM Shillong, the institution where he breathed his last.

In a way, he was leading by example. It was his contribution to the movement What Can I Give. As a teacher he believed that these new institutions deserved all the help they could get, and he was always there to support them.

On the flight to Indore, we were allotted seats in the last row. It was a small plane, and hence there were no middle seats. Dr Kalam sat by the window and I by the aisle. The airline staff had ensured Dr Kalam boarded the plane after all the other passengers, and that too through the rear gate, so no one would know of his presence.

The plane soon took off, and after a while the seat-belt signs were turned off. Dr Kalam had a habit of unbuckling his seat belt as soon as the lights went off because he had to reach for his handbag, which he kept at his feet. His bag always had numerous papers and books, and he never wasted a second to get to reading them.

This time, as soon as the seat-belt signs were turned off, a little girl stepped into the aisle from the row in front of us. She was clutching a packet of nachos in her hands. She had barely learnt to walk and was going around offering her nachos to every passenger on the plane. Each time someone reached out for one, she would chuckle in delight.

By the time she came to us, the packet was almost empty. Of course, she did not recognize Dr Kalam. She wiped her nose with her free hand and said, '*Lo, kha lo. Achha hai.*' (Here, eat. It is delicious.) It was heartening to see a two-year-old willingly give away her prized possession. Dr Kalam immediately reached out and took a small piece.

Putting it in his mouth, he said, '*Bohot achha! Kya naam hai?*' (Very good, what is your name?)

'Manvi,' the girl replied.

Hearing the conversation, her mother, who was sitting right in front of me, turned around. She was dumbstruck to find her daughter in conversation with the former President of India. She could only manage a stunned 'wow!' Once she had regained her composure, she told us a little about her daughter. It turned out that her daughter, two-year-old Manvi, was a regular 'giver'. She always shared her food with everyone, even with complete strangers.

'I am impressed with Manvi's attitude. She is indeed being given a great education by her mother. So I congratulate you. I am sure she will grow up to be a wonderful person,' said Dr Kalam.

Elated at receiving such appreciation from the President himself, she requested for a picture of Manvi with Dr Kalam.

'Of course. I will be glad. Come,' he said, beckoning to Manvi.

I got up from my seat and offered it to her.

The innocent child, unaware of Dr Kalam's stature, sat down next to him confidently. Her mother, on the other hand, kept fumbling with her phone and could hardly click a picture properly. So I offered to take it on my phone and send it to her.

'Smile! three . . . two . . . one . . .' Dr Kalam urged the child. He always said that the countdown should be in reverse. It was more scientific and made more sense. 'If you count upwards, I won't know where you will stop and click!'

Just then we were asked to prepare for landing. Manvi was still sitting in my seat, chatting with Dr Kalam. She was looking for leftover crumbs in her empty packet of nachos and sharing whatever she found with her new friend. But since the plane was about to begin its descent, her mother took her back to their seat.

When the plane landed at the airport and the gates were thrown open, Manvi's mother gave me her email address so that I could send her the picture I had taken on my phone. I was sure that Dr Kalam would share this incident on his social media. Within five minutes of leaving the airport, Dr Kalam started talking about Manvi. 'What a wonderful child! She is an ambassador of What Can I Give. It is a wonderful trait in a child—to share something that she likes, and so happily . . . I learnt a lesson from her today.'

'And what is that?' I knew that it was a great experience, but I wondered what *he* had learnt from it.

'You see, I learnt that the ability to share what one loves the most is innate; it cannot be taught by religion or books. We just need to reach out to the child inside us. We have to speak about this incident.'

'You mean tweet?' I asked.

'Yes. Do it, I say,' he insisted.

I did as told. The tweet read:

In flight to Indore. Met 2yr old Manvi. She kept offering her nachos to every1 on flight. Impressive spirit of sharing.

This tweet was picked up by the media, and thus, the next day, the whole world was ready to learn the lesson of sharing from a little girl.

When I saw the news, I showed it to Dr Kalam.

'Her attitude deserves to be celebrated and replicated. We did something good by writing about her,' he said.

Dr Kalam believed that every good deed must be made known, no matter whom the lesson came from.

25

Respecting and Celebrating Differences

Dr Kalam had a simple and consistent diet, comprising largely south Indian vegetarian food—dosa, idli, sambar, dal, slightly overcooked rice and occasionally chapatis. That would be his breakfast, lunch and dinner. Even his last lunch at the Guwahati airport was a simple meal of dosa and sambar.

He was very particular about his meal timings. So we devised a formula that would enable him to always eat on time—T minus 2 and T minus 4. It was simple. If we had to start work at, say, 8.30 a.m., Dr Kalam would wake up four hours earlier. He would just have tea and a couple of Marigold biscuits. At T minus 2—6.30 a.m.—he would have his breakfast. This rule would stand regardless of what time he went to sleep at night. It was remarkable that even in his eighties he could be so disciplined. It didn't matter whether he slept for just three or four hours and had an extremely hectic day ahead; he would always follow this rule without fail.

He would ensure that all his accompanying staff ate with him. He loved the low-oil Kerala version of dosa, and he made sure that his chef in Delhi learnt how to make it. No meal was ever complete without plain yogurt—he called it *thayir*, in Tamil—a lot of lemon slices and pickle. If the lemon was missing, as it often was on our trips, then he would tell us to 'ask for the cut-fellows', which meant that he wanted us to check with the hosts if there were any lemons.

It took me a while to figure out why he never asked for these lemons directly. It was because he did not want to disappoint the hosts by making a direct request that they might not be able to fulfil at that moment. If the request came from one of his staffers or co-diners privately then it would not be as embarrassing for the host—in case they had to say no.

Throughout our meal, he would keep asking us whether we liked the food. I am particularly fond of apples, something he was aware of. So, whenever he found apples in the welcome fruit-basket at hotels, he would pick them out and ask me to take them along, saying, 'You are an apple fellow, take your friends with you.'

I remember this one visit to Scotland in 2014, where the chef and his team did not know how to make dosas. So we improvised. We instructed them to make extra-thin pancakes without any sugar or syrup. Lo and behold, the Kerala dosa was ready in Edinburgh! Dr Kalam said, 'It tastes 80 per cent Trivandrum and 20 per cent Edinburgh!'

He disliked paneer, and many of our hosts assumed otherwise, but he never complained and would quietly eat a small portion of it. But he was very particular about the flavour of his tea. In fact, quite often he'd request to make his own tea on flights!

We usually stayed at the Raj Bhavans (residence of the Governor of the state) when travelling to state capitals within India. Sometimes the staff would try to serve us food separately, in our respective rooms. He would always veto it and insist that all his associates be brought to the same dining table as him. Once, he explained the reason for this. 'I know that if they give you guys food separately, they will not give you all the nice things.' He would insist on this dining-table rule, and sometimes even the host Governor would join us for lunch or dinner. It was such small acts of deep compassion that made him so popular.

A tricky situation arose during lunch at the Jaipur Raj Bhavan one time. We had come back from an event and were in separate rooms when the Raj Bhavan staff asked me and another member of the team to join in for lunch. When we reached the lunch table we realized that they had served only us, while Dr Kalam had been taken to a separate room where he could have lunch with the Governor. Of course, we were perfectly fine with it, but it was the only time that we had eaten separately on a trip together. Later, when we met after our separate lunches, the first question he asked was, 'Did they give you good food?' We nodded an affirmative. He was not convinced, however, and quizzed us on the items we had eaten. When he realized that we had been offered the same menu as him, he was finally satisfied.

* * *

I was born in the city of Lucknow. Once known as Oudh, this historic city is now famous for three marvels—food, music and architecture—all of which have been heavily influenced by the Muslim emperors who ruled over this place for centuries, till the British took over in 1857. I grew up in a Hindu family, and like many other people from similar backgrounds, I too am a non-vegetarian foodie.

My teacher, Dr Kalam, was born into a Muslim family in Rameswaram—considered one of the holiest sites in India by Hindus. For the greater part of his life, he had been a strict vegetarian. This situation gave rise to many interesting and insightful incidents in my life.

In my early days with him, I could not muster the courage to order non-vegetarian food on a flight together. I did not know whether he would be okay with me eating non-veg, sitting right beside him. This went on for a while till someone in our office mentioned to him that I loved eating meat.

The next day at lunch, he sprang a surprise on me. 'I have something special that you should smash!'

'Smash' was his way of saying 'eat well'. Often he would ask, 'Are you guys smashing well?' to see if we were eating well.

He called for Chellapa, the person who cooked and served us all food. He brought out a steaming bowl of egg curry for me. 'I did not know you smash non-veg food. You should have told me. My fellows make funny things very well,' he said, pointing at Chellapa.

By 'funny things', he meant non-vegetarian food items.

'I say, smash!' he said.

I was slightly embarrassed and could not find an appropriate response.

Sensing my hesitation, he said, 'Don't worry. Have it. People are not judged by what's on their plate, but what's in their character.' And then, to remove my doubt forever, he turned around and said, 'Chellapa, whenever possible, make some funny things for your friend here.'

Encouraged by this, I asked him, 'Sir, everyone in your family is non-vegetarian. Children generally pick up habits from the grown-ups around them. Why did you choose to be vegetarian? Was it some teacher who inspired you?'

He then told me the most inspiring story ever. 'You see, I became vegetarian for financial reasons. I was not a vegetarian by birth. When I joined MIT for my course in Aeronautics, the fee was very high and we weren't very well off. So we had to really adjust a lot to accommodate my expenses, and we had to borrow money from others. Somehow we managed to arrange the fees for my course. I also had to live in a hostel and had to choose from three messes—a high-end, multi-cuisine one for the rich students, a regular non-vegetarian one and a strictly vegetarian one, which was also the cheapest. I did not want to put more pressure on my parents, so I readily joined the vegetarian mess without telling them. For those four years I did not have the money to eat out, so I only ate at the mess. I thought I would start eating non-vegetarian food once I started earning. But something strange happened—I began to like vegetarian food. So even after I graduated and started earning, I remained a vegetarian. Now it's been more than six decades since I tasted "funny things" and I like it this way.'

It was a profoundly interesting conversation. It revealed his sensitive and logical nature. It showed that he could make difficult decisions, even going as far as breaking lifelong habits, when he really needed to.

From that lunch onwards, a non-vegetarian dish would be made or ordered especially for me, whenever possible. Dr Kalam would pull the vegetables towards himself and push the 'funny things' towards me. Then he would draw an imaginary line on the table with his finger and joke, 'That is your territory and this is mine.' As for the dessert, he would push it towards my territory and say, 'You eat double!' And he would add, 'Then you will become double.'

There would be frequent mix-ups on our travels abroad because of our names. On one such trip, the hotel staff gave Dr Kalam the vegetarian dish and me the non-vegetarian one. Since the meat was minced, it was difficult to identify which was which. We were about to start eating when we noticed the greens in my plate, which were curiously missing from Dr Kalam's. We paused and checked our food carefully and then realized the error that had been made. Dr Kalam was unperturbed, though. He laughed and said, 'You, fellow, would have made me eat funny things. Here, let us exchange our plates.'

That was it. Not a word was said about the incident again. Dr Kalam believed in finding solutions, instead of making a big hue and cry over small issues like these. He insisted that non-vegetarian food be made available for his staff, whenever possible. He was considerate of other people's habits and customs and believed that the essence of a harmonious society lies in respecting other cultures. He believed that tolerance is the secret to building a beautiful world.

In one of his speeches in 2009, he said, 'A beautiful society [can] be achieved if there is more:

1. Tolerance for people's opinions
2. Tolerance for different cultures
3. Tolerance for others' beliefs
4. Tolerance for each person's style

A great and mature society is where individuals celebrate and respect difference.'

Srijan Pal Singh

Today when I read about the bans and controversies regarding what people should or should not eat, I am reminded of Dr Kalam and how I received profound lessons in tolerance right at our dinner table.

26

Picture-Perfect!

In July 2014, Dr Kalam accepted the invitation to attend the golden jubilee celebrations at Dr Ambedkar College, in Nagpur. When the college publicized the news locally, we received a request from another school—Jeevodaya Education Society, the college of special education in Nagpur. They wrote to us saying that many of their students had grown up to be successful, self-reliant professionals. They requested Dr Kalam to visit the school as it would boost the morale of these children and inspire them to overcome obstacles.

Dr Kalam followed a particular rule while accepting invitations from institutions. If he was visiting some well-known institution, then he would follow it up with a visit to a smaller institution. It was his way of connecting to underprivileged citizens and encouraging them to dream big. Jeevodaya Education Society fitted the bill.

This special school was established in 1989 by the Archdiocese of Nagpur. A diocese is like an administrative district of a church—the area where it operates. This particular school has been catering to the needs of disabled people of their region since its inception.

When we reached the school we were greeted by the headmaster and a few teachers, who took us around the premises. It was a beautiful sight. All the classrooms were decorated with colourful paper-cuttings, drawings and other craftwork made by the students.

The auditorium was modestly sized, but it had an unusually large stage. Dr Kalam, the headmaster and the senior teachers were seated in the centre of the stage. And I was sitting right behind Dr Kalam. The anchor, a young teacher, listed the agenda for the programme and introduced everyone.

Dr Kalam always took down notes while other people delivered their speeches and lectures. He even made notes when the emcee took the mic. He would then pass them to me, and I would pick some sentences from these notes and type them on my laptop. Those lines would then get projected on his reading screen and he would start his speech with those words. This was our way of connecting with the audience and our fellow speakers.

That day, while sitting on stage and waiting for the anchor to finish his introduction, Dr Kalam turned back and gestured to me. When I got up and leaned towards him, he said, 'You know, this teacher is also a product of this school. We must greet him separately.' In fact, the principal, who was sitting with us, told us that many of the other teachers were also ex-students of that school—as children, they had also suffered from conditions similar to what their students were suffering from today.

When Dr Kalam got up to speak, he first approached the emcee and greeted him. He said, 'I am sure nobody would understand the potential of the children here better than you would. Well done. You did a great job with the programme today, and I am sure you are a wonderful teacher too.'

The students were brimming with energy when Dr Kalam began addressing them. They listened with rapt attention as he spoke about how 'our minds are stronger than diamonds'. He had two poems for the occasion, and he made the students recite one of them—

> When God is with us, who can be against.
> We will win, win, win with our mighty will.
> Our minds are stronger than diamonds.
> We are all God's children,
> We will win, win, win with our mighty will.
> When God is with us, who can be against.

The other one was reserved for the parents present. He set them some 'homework'—he urged them to recite it in their respective mother tongues, together with their children, every night before going to bed.

I am not alone,
God is always with me.
If God is for me,
Who can be against.
I sought the Lord, He heard me,
Delivered me from all fears.
Divine light penetrated into me
And cured my pain in body and soul.
Divine beauty enters into me,
And blossoms into happiness.
When God is for me,
Who can be against.

After his lecture, Dr Kalam answered a few questions. Then the headmaster asked a very special child to come up on stage. A young girl with a sheet of paper clutched in her hand walked up to Dr Kalam amidst loud cheers. As she handed him the paper, she said, '*Maine banaya*.' (I made it.) It was a pencil sketch of Dr Kalam. He immediately shook her hand and asked her her name.

'My name is . . .' she paused for a moment and then said, 'Khalilullah.'

Khalilullah suffered from Down's syndrome, a rare condition, which occurs in less than 0.1 per cent of newborns. It severely inhibits growth and development, often stunting one's IQ to less than 50. But that did not stop Khalilullah from picking up a pencil and making a remarkable portrait of Dr Kalam.

He asked her how much time it had taken her to make it.

'I made it several times,' she replied. 'But it did not come out well. So I made it again. It took me many days to complete this.'

The end result was wonderful.

Usually, when Dr Kalam was given such presents he handed it over to his team for safekeeping. This time, however, as Khalilullah went back to her seat, he folded the paper and tucked it inside his coat pocket. He rarely ever did something like that. He smiled at me, and I instantly knew that Khalilullah had touched his heart deeply.

Later, when we were alone in the car, I asked him to show me the sketch. We both looked at it carefully. After a small silence he said, 'You, fellow, you know, this is my favourite sketch.'

'Why did you keep it in your pocket?'

'Because you fellows might lose it,' he said.

Now I had to protest. 'When have I ever lost anything?'

'But this is very valuable, you see. So I need to be extra careful.'

'Why?' I probed further.

'Imagine the pains the girl must have taken to draw it again and again, till she was satisfied. In her mind, this is the pinnacle of perfection and that quest is always a struggle, I can tell you this. Its value is in the effort that has gone into creating it! So, this is very valuable. You got it?'

As the car reached our guest house, I said, 'Okay. But will you lend me the picture for just a minute? I am sure you want me to share it on your social media.'

Handing it to me, he said with a smile, 'But I want it back immediately.'

I tweeted a photo of the sketch along with this message:

This sketch was gifted2me in Nagpur by Khalilullah. A young girl suffering from Down's syndrome. Thnku my friend.

* * *

Dr Kalam's eighty-fourth birth anniversary was on 15 October 2015—the first one after his demise. Starting with an appeal on social media, tens of thousands of Dr Kalam's fans changed their profile picture to the sketch made by Khalilullah. This was both a mark of respect for Dr Kalam and also a salute to the love he had for children. Some of his ardent fans still use the sketch as their profile pictures.

27

When You Trust Your Ability, You Should Not Fear Taking Risks

In 2014, I was toying with the idea of starting a technological enterprise to develop low-cost, multi-utility robots. One particular possibility was to develop an automatic aerial machine, popularly known as a drone, retrofitted with multiple robotic arms, cameras and other devices, which would lend the robots the ability to lift and drop objects. The project needed a significantly high capital investment.

Most of the drones available in the market at the time were imported from China. So a similar Indian product was sure to grab eyeballs. But I couldn't find any investors for this unique project and my own resources were not sufficient to meet the needed capital. As a result of intensive research, my team and I were confident that we could manufacture such multi-purpose drones successfully. But without any financial backing from investors, it would have been a huge gamble to move ahead with the project. I had discussed this project with Dr Kalam at the beginning of the research itself. As a scientist he had a keen interest in anything that could fly and he'd guided us through the entire planning stage. If he came across any relevant material on drones, while reading books or newspapers, he would mark that portion and send it over to my work table.

When we were at the critical juncture of deciding how to go ahead with the project, I was inevitably nervous. And as I would always do, I went to discuss this with Dr Kalam. I told him about the possibilities that this project had and about my helpless situation. My team had great plans for the drones—our drones would help save the lives of soldiers in the armed forces, they would help in rescue missions and would even help with the targeted delivery of pesticides. He was surprised to learn that no big investors were coming forward to fund this project.

After a brief silence he asked, 'So why do you think there are no investors for such a machine?'

'Because . . .' I was not sure of the reason, but I tried, 'they are not sure whether the device will fly, let alone perform the intended tasks.'

'But what about your design team?' he asked.

'We are sure of the design. It will fly. We would have liked to test our design with a smaller prototype first, but considering our financial situation, we can't afford to make either the prototype or the actual device.'

He understood. 'That is always the dilemma of an inventor. You know that what you have made will work, but other people, sometimes influential people, doubt you. Funny fellows they are! This is where inventors and entrepreneurs hit a brick wall. Now you can either choose to break the wall or turn around and leave . . .' Then, pausing for a moment, he continued, 'I have seen this many times . . . let me tell you a story.

'It was in May 1989. Our grandest missile project so far, Agni, was on the verge of being tested. We had faced numerous technological denials, our scientists had literally been thrown out of foreign countries on a day's notice and everybody was keeping an ominous eye on our activities. We were hoping to swim against an international tide, created by the most powerful nations, and win.

'Despite all the limitations, we finally managed to develop our own, 100 per cent indigenous ballistic missile—a world-class weapon system which could match the ones being used by the developed countries. Only the final test on the missile stood between us and our place in the prestigious list of nations fielding ballistic missiles. As the director of the Defence Research and Development Laboratory (DRDL), this was my team's most important project, which would give India one of the leading missile technologies in the world.

'As the designated date for testing, 22 May 1989, drew closer, we were filled with nervous excitement. We had decided to conduct the tests in the Chandipur-based Integrated Test Range (ITR), Odisha. All our team members were excited, the scene was abuzz with ideas, thoughts and sometimes concerns, all leading to many long and passionate discussions. Everybody was committed to doing their best to make this project a success. We had been abandoned by the powerful nations during our programme but we were determined to bounce back. Our efforts and innovations had borne great fruits, and using Computer Fluid Dynamics (CFD) and simulations we had almost reinvented the entire design process of a missile.

'As the leader of the project I had other worries too. The United States had got an inkling of our project. A few years back, when we were working on this same missile system in Frankfurt, the US had managed to evict us from there. And now the US did not know for sure what we had accomplished but they were getting suspicious. The newly elected President, George H.W. Bush, had just assumed office and, like his predecessor, President Ronald Reagan, he too was willing to use all his diplomatic forces to stop India from acquiring the coveted long-range missile technology. Just a few weeks before the intended tests, we started getting reports of the US spy satellites that were locked on Chandipur, trying to gather information.

'The exact date of the missile test was known only to a handful of people. We all knew that with the satellites snooping around, there was a potential risk of our plans being found out well in advance. Then there were reports of the US government and intelligence already expressing their ill ease with whatever was afoot in Chandipur. We knew that after winning the battle against technology denial, we were now running a race against time and facing an imminent diplomatic manoeuvre that could put paid to all our efforts.

'It was 3 a.m. on the 22nd, the test date. We were still in the missile-assembling area, fitting the final pieces of the first Agni together, when the hotline started ringing. There were no mobile phones in those days, and even long-distance calling over wired telephones was a time-consuming process. So for all critical communications, we had installed a hotline number, which only the top-level offices could use. A hotline call at 3 a.m., four or five hours prior to the launch, could not be a good sign.

'Putting the receiver to my ear, I said, "Hello." On the other end was Dr V.S. Arunachalam. He was the scientific adviser to the defence minister and the chief of DRDO, and my immediate boss. Without preamble, and in a sombre voice, he said, "Mr Sheshan wants to talk to you. Be ready. I will call back in five minutes." The conversation ended and left me with hundreds of questions. Mr T.N. Sheshan, a renowned bureaucrat, was the Cabinet Secretary to the then Prime Minister, Rajiv Gandhi. A brilliant man, full of ideas, he was the senior-most bureaucrat in the nation and was known for handling complex affairs. I wondered why he wanted to talk to me at that hour.

'As advised by my boss, I waited near the hotline, occasionally shifting my eyes to the large wall clock and then back towards the missile parts that were being ferried around enthusiastically by my team. Five minutes passed, then ten, and then fifteen. The wait was excruciating.

'The phone went off again. "Sir!" I immediately picked up the receiver. "Good moring, Kalam." It was Mr Sheshan on the other end. I reciprocated, and that was the end of the niceties. He got straight to the point.

'"Where are we on Agni?" he asked, and then continued without waiting for me to answer. "We are under tremendous pressure from the US and the North Atlantic Treaty Organization (NATO) to delay any impending missile testing. There are strong diplomatic influences at play." Then almost immediately, he followed with his first question, "Kalam! Where are we on Agni?"

'Honestly, as a project director this was a difficult question to answer. Of course, we were doing well with Agni. But his question was implying something else. He was also asking for my suggestion on whether the Agni testing should be delayed.

'For the next few seconds my mind raced. There were intelligence reports that US satellites had their gazes fixed on us. I knew that the US was putting increasing pressure on the Prime Minister and his office to delay the launch. Worse, there were reports that Chandipur would be faced with terrible weather in the next few days.

'Then there was my team—hard-working, determined young men and women, whom we had hand-picked for this assignment about a decade ago. They had been through everything—technology denials, evictions from other nations, tight budgets, media pressure and frustrating setbacks due to lack of critical apparatus. Their triumph was right in front of them—the magnificent Agni, proudly sporting the tri-colour. India was going to begin a new chapter in its scientific progress and strategic power. Should I stand down and overwrite this chapter with delay?

'Strictly speaking, the missile was still at bay. The project could have been stopped and shelved for a while. We had the storage capacity for Agni. Maybe we would win the war of diplomacy one day. Maybe someday in the near future we would find a space and time in the international scenario to test Agni safely. Maybe this was the day for patience, the day for accepting perhaps a small defeat and the day for waiting for a better moment.

'Or, perhaps it was not a time to wait and watch, but to act and cherish. I calculated all my variables and then, clearing my throat, I said, "Sir, the missile is at a point of no return. We cannot turn back on the test now. It is too late." I expected a debate and a barrage of questions from my boss and Mr Sheshan. But to my surprise, as the clock struck four and the sun started appearing on the horizon, Mr Sheshan just said, "Okay," and then paused to take a deep breath, "go ahead."

'That was all I needed. With a "thank you", I immediately replaced the receiver, hoping that it would not ring again till we had completed the test. My wish was fulfilled.

'Three hours later, we launched the Agni missile system—a missile system which was made in India, which had never been tested in wind tunnels, which was made with the simplest screws to control complex flights. The weapon system which would become the pride of our nation was tested on 22 May 1989. It was a flawless execution of the hopes and aspirations of a bunch of young scientists who could not be deterred by any force on this planet. We had created history.

'The next day, there was a storm in Chandipur that partially destroyed our testing facility. But we all knew that we had already won the race for Agni.'

* * *

It was a moving story of the risk that Dr Kalam had taken in his career to save the missile. After hearing this story I asked him, 'But what if the test had failed that morning?'

'Oh. Then I would have been in deep trouble. But I trusted in the work we had done on Agni. I strongly believed that if I did not fail Agni, then Agni would not fail me. When you trust your ability, you should not be afraid of taking risks.'

This story inspired us to move ahead with our much more humble drone-robot project. We decided to go all out on the very first prototype. We gathered our resources and also garnered some support from friends. Instead of testing with a four-propeller drone, we went straight for a much larger six-propeller drone.

Our drone was successful in the very first go, much like Agni. We named it 'Wings of Fire' after its inspiration.

When Dr Kalam was told about the success of the multi-purpose drone, he was thrilled. He was eager to see it fly. So, on 23 December 2014, Dr Kalam visited Lucknow where the Wings of Fire was launched for the first time in his presence and with his blessings. After the flight was completed amidst a cheering audience, Dr Kalam said, 'I am happy to see that you fellows trust your ability. It is beautiful.'

28

These Are My People

On each of our trips, especially within the country, we got to witness some unique sights whenever we left the guest house.

An array of people of all age groups would assemble in the hopes of seeing and meeting Dr Kalam. There would be little girls in school uniforms, waiting to give him roses, older children would be carrying one of his books, hoping to get an autograph and the more creative ones would have brought a colourful drawing of Dr Kalam or of one his missiles.

On the other end of the age spectrum, there would even be people who were well into their eighties. These octogenarians often had some unexecuted ideas that they wanted to share with Dr Kalam. They would wait for Dr Kalam with printed and laminated sheets which contained explanations of their ideas that they believed could change the nation. Often we came across some truly interesting people.

Once, in Sarangpur, one such unscheduled visitor turned out to be more than ninety years old; he was a renowned freedom fighter who had walked with none other than Gandhiji! Then in Allahabad, we met a retired railway employee who had invented an improved pattern of laying railway tracks which could make train rides smoother.

Usually there would be thirty to forty such unexpected guests waiting all along the hallway and near the car. The less fortunate ones were stopped at the main gate itself, where they would wait just to catch a glimpse of their Missile Man.

The very old and the very young would be made to sit while Dr Kalam greeted and shook hands with the people standing in queues. He would often stop to click pictures with his admirers. He had strictly forbidden his staff from turning away anyone who had come to meet him. He insisted on meeting everyone, even if it was for just ten seconds.

While leaving in his bulletproof car, Dr Kalam would instruct the driver to drive 'dead-slow'. As the car rolled past, the crowd would cheer and wave at him. Some people would take out their mobiles and click pictures. If he ever saw anyone waving at him, especially children, he would stop whatever work he was doing and wave back. The children would smile at him happily.

Dr Kalam strongly believed that he belonged to the people, and these little gestures were to show them that he was truly one of them.

During one of our trips to Guwahati in 2011, we were hard-pressed for time—the lecture he was to deliver was not fully ready yet and we were going through it on our way to the event. Meanwhile, groups of people standing on the road kept waving at him and each time Dr Kalam would stop his work and wave back. When this happened for the third time, I couldn't help saying, 'Sir, you are getting distracted again and again.'

He said, 'These are my people. I have lived a similar life. You see, a person very rarely gets the power to bring smiles on the faces of others. Think about it! Notice how they smile when they see me wave back. Being noticed, being relevant is a basic human quest, one which brings happiness. They will go home smiling, and they will tell their families about this and then the whole family will be happy. With just a wave and a smile, we have the power to make so many people happy. Is it not worth a second of distraction? In life, if you have the power to make someone smile, never refrain from taking the time out to do so. Life will gloriously pay you back for the time you invest.'

I absorbed this powerful advice. Indeed, the essence of noble living is in spreading smiles all around. While the lesson was still sinking in, he interrupted my chain of thought. 'Let's get back to work. So what was it that you wanted to add to the lecture?'

Life went back to normal, but with an extra smile.

* * *

In the last week of February 2010, Dr Kalam visited the district of Kolhapur in Maharashtra. This visit was initiated by

Professor Samar Datta and me. Professor Datta is a renowned academician from IIM Ahmedabad, and was my teacher back when I was a student there. Our primary goal was the initiation of a programme under PURA (a brainchild of Dr Kalam) in an area known as Warana in Kolhapur.

There was a sugar and dairy cooperative at the PURA complex in Warana, along with a chain of over fifty women-run superstores, one state-of-the-art sugar mill, a dairy plant, numerous chilling plants, training centres and schools, a couple of colleges, a hospital and even a dedicated bank. They also had thriving sugar-cane cultivations and support for animal husbandry. It was a remarkable project which was benefiting over three lakh people, ensuring that absolutely no one in the area was below the poverty line. This project was a result of the hard work of many generations, and all the products of their individual efforts had been brought together by Professor Datta under the single banner of Warana PURA.

I had worked with Professor Datta on this project as a student and continued as a professional since 2008. In 2010, when our work was finally completed, we invited Dr Kalam to inaugurate the project. We'd set 24 February as the date for his visit to this rather remote part of India, which was nevertheless a vibrant economy.

We arrived there around noon—it was a ninety-minute car ride from the Kolhapur airport. Once we reached the venue the overjoyed villagers showed up in large numbers.

We were scheduled to visit the community hospital, attend an event at the college that was managed by the sugar-cane farmers, visit the dairy and drive by the sugar factory—which was in operation and hence unsafe for a visit. Finally, Dr Kalam was to declare the Warana PURA as a mission and address about 50,000 farmers.

After completing the first few tasks we reached the sugar factory, which was at the heart of our programme. It was about 3 p.m. on a hot sunny day. While we were in the middle of our scheduled drive-by, we saw groups of sugar-cane farmers waiting with their bullock carts. They were in a queue to get their sugar cane weighed before delivering them to the factory. It is an anxious wait for the farmers because the results of this weighing would determine the value of their year-long hard work and toil.

They saw us in our cars and looked on curiously. I was with Dr Kalam in the bulletproof Ambassador, with the local manager sitting in the front and explaining the entire operational process of the mill to us. Dr Kalam was not paying the manager his full attention. His focus was on the farmers outside. Some of them were standing with their bullocks, giving the animals water, and the others were neatly rearranging the sugar canes piled in the cart.

Rural India presents a very vivid sight during the months of harvest—farmers swell with pride when they look at their harvest and yet they are nervous about the money it will fetch them. A farmer is forced to wonder if his produce will bring in enough cash to cover his debts, ensure his children's education, pay for his basic necessities and let him make that special purchase he has been wanting to make for his family.

Often there is a thin line that farmers, who form 50 per cent of the nation's workforce, have to tread. A high yield may seem like good news at a cursory glance but could lead to prices crashing and processing overloads at the agro-factories, which could lead to long waiting periods. Even after seven decades of being in the political spotlight, the farmers of India still suffer severe anxiety during the seasons of harvest. The farmers in Warana PURA were, perhaps, slightly better off—given that the sugar mill was partly owned by them under the cooperative model.

While we completed our drive around the mill, Dr Kalam kept observing the farmers. A moment later he looked like he had made up his mind about something. He asked, 'These farmers are the producers and the owners of the mill, right?'

'Yes, sir. Eighteen thousand farmers own this mill,' replied the mill representative, who was also with us.

'These are my people,' Dr Kalam said. 'I want to talk to them.'

The mill representative was surprised. 'Yes, sir. We will be meeting them in the grand function later.'

'No, I want to meet them now.'

I immediately asked the driver to stop the car. Dr Kalam pushed open the heavily armoured door and walked towards the farmers. The policemen who had rushed out of their vehicles were finding it hard to keep pace with the eighty-year-old President. The farmers looked happy to see him but were also clearly alarmed by the policemen running towards them as well. Dr Kalam reached them and asked them how they harvested their produce, what their aspirations were and what they were doing to ensure a happy future for their children. One of the local policemen acted as translator. After this impromptu meeting, Dr Kalam came with a mission for all of them. He asked them, '*Aap log mere saath shapath lenge?*' (Will you take an oath with me?)

The farmers cheered in agreement and repeated after Dr Kalam:

1. Agriculture is a noble mission. I will add value and grow produce.
2. Land and water are our greatest resources. I will protect and preserve them.
3. I will help build all the farm ponds in our area, so that water will be available throughout the year.
4. I realize that for soil enrichment I will have to switch over to multi-cropping.
5. I will use technology and good agricultural practices for improving productivity.
6. I will take up organic agriculture.
7. I will convert agricultural waste into wealth in the form of energy and organic fertilizers.

8. Children are our future; I will educate my children without any discrimination between boys and girls.
9. I will not waste hard-earned money on drinking and gambling.

He then thanked the farmers for their hard work and said, 'Now you fellows come around. Only the farmers. Click. three . . . two . . . one . . .'

He added with a smile, 'You fellows have taken an oath. Now if you don't follow it, I will catch you. I also have a photograph of all of you.' The sugar-cane farmers laughed cheerfully. Dr Kalam had become one of their own.

Favourite Sport

Dr Kalam never really watched TV. But he was still a cricket fan. He would ask me about cricket scores when we travelled. His favourite cricketers were Dhoni and Sachin. If I told him India was not doing well in a particular match, he would calmly respond, 'Just keep watching! Our captain will come and do something unique. You just watch.'

But it would not be right to assume that cricket was his favourite sport. I had once asked him directly, 'So is cricket your favourite sport?'

Srijan Pal Singh

He had replied, 'No. It is at second place. My
favourite sport is badminton. I loved that sport when
I was a kid.'

———————— ✳ ————————

29

Live to Give

The people who visited 10, Rajaji Marg to meet Dr Kalam were inevitably asked one question:

'Have you met my friend Arjuna? Let me introduce you to him. He is a wonderful fellow.'

Then he would escort the guest to the front garden, where Arjuna stood—tall and majestic like the warrior he had been named after, the long years proudly etched on his body.

Dr Kalam would then say, 'This fellow is very old. Hundred-and-ten years old. He must have seen so much, imagine—Gandhiji, Nehru, the freedom wars and India's rising story. He holds an entire section of history his heart. He is my best friend.'

Arjuna would wave back at Dr Kalam gently, its large branches swaying gracefully. The people who have seen it have always been tempted to take a selfie with it.

Arjuna was almost three decades older than Dr Kalam. He was the most special occupant of 10, Rajaji Marg, loved and respected by the owner of the house.

Dr Kalam would walk up to him every day and they would exchange their thoughts silently. No one knew what they communicated, in what language, but we all knew that they made each other wiser. Dr Kalam would often thank Arjuna for taking care of 10, Rajaji Marg through the ages and for helping so many flowers and plants grow under his care. Arjuna was also the official bee-keeper of the house.

One day in 2012, while Dr Kalam and I were in the garden, I asked him, 'What is so special about Arjuna? Why do you admire him so much?'

He looked at me, puzzled. Then he said, 'Because Arjuna lives to give and anyone who lives to give needs to be venerated. Arjuna's mission in life has been "What can I give, what can I give, what can I give?" That is why he is standing so proudly and happily at such an age.'

I could feel Arjuna, the 110 year-old Terminalia tree, smile behind us.

* * *

The conversation did not stop there. Dr Kalam gave me a task one day.

'Can you determine how many lives Arjuna supports?' he asked.

I was puzzled. It was an unexpected challenge.

'Go ahead, find out,' he said.

So I walked up to the giant tree and counted the thick rings of runners around the trunk. Runners are smaller plants that cannot support themselves and so spread themselves around the trunks of large and stronger trees like Arjuna.

One, two, three . . . eleven. Bingo. Eleven rings.

I came back with my answer. 'Sir, it supports eleven rings and of course, it gives out oxygen.'

'Oh. You missed the nests. Look again.'

So I went back to Arjuna. This task was difficult because the tree was heavy with foliage, which carefully shielded its inner branches. I managed to count about twelve nests.

I went back. 'Sir, it supports eleven rings, twelve nests, and gives oxygen.'

'You missed something again. Come with me.' This time he walked back towards Arjuna with me. Pointing down at the base of the trunk, he said, 'You missed this. Didn't you?'

There it was. Hidden in the dense bushes, growing around the base of the trunk was a peacock's nest, and a beautiful peahen was laying her eggs in there.

'Yes, I missed it.'

'You know why? Because we often look for solutions that are above us and that makes the solutions look more magnificent. Our mind points us that way. Thus we ignore the inspiration that comes from below, from the ground level. You missed, the largest nest, with the prettiest birds in it, because it was lying on the ground—at the base, around the roots. Diamonds are found the depths of the earth, and not at the height of the sky.'

A few weeks later, the nest became alive with the chirping of five little chicks. Dr Kalam asked me if I knew what a baby peacock was called. And before I could google it, he gave them a name—'Pea-children'.

The pea-children became a part of the 10, Rajaji Marg family. Dr Kalam would regularly ensure that they were fed in the courtyard, which was near the dining room. While we had lunch at the table, he would get birdfeed laid out at the courtyard for the pea-children. And the pea-children would flock to it hungrily.

'We have more guests for lunch. Now they will always come here for their lunch happily, even when we are not there. You just keep watching; they will come, and come just on time, regardless of anything,' he would say.

Of course, soon the pea-children were joined by many other birds—pigeons, parrots and crows. This established a tradition which continued for years to come. Even when Dr Kalam went out of town, those birds were served their food. He would remind his staff to feed them whenever he was gone for a long time. And he made it a point to check on them whenever he returned from his trip.

When I returned to 10, Rajaji Marg after Dr Kalam's death, the fact that he would never again eat in that dining room across the courtyard sunk in. But the birds are still fed, like they used to be in his time. The birds will always be fed, in his honour.

30

Goodness Is in the Colours of Compassion and Empathy

In 2011, my mode of transport around Delhi used to be a motorbike; it was old and an unusual green in colour, but incredibly fuel efficient. One Saturday morning, I arrived at the office at my usual time, 9.30 a.m. In those days I used to stay about 5 kilometres away from the office. When I reached I saw a man standing in front of the large iron gate. He was in the middle of an animated conversation with the security person. He was an old man, with a rough beard and long, frizzy grey hair which was mostly hidden under his turban. I got down from my bike and approached him. He was carrying a long, slender stick with him; when I looked at his face I realized that he was totally blind. A little kid was hiding behind him and peeping at us. This kid was about ten years old. The child seemed afraid of the policemen around but the old man continued to talk confidently. He was saying, 'Let me meet my President for one minute. I will bless you.'

When I went closer to him he immediately sensed my presence. I asked him, 'Baba, what do you want?'

His enthusiasm peaked when he heard me. He replied, 'I have come from Mathura. I have no one with me, except Javed. He is my only grandson. My son died of cholera and my daughter-in-law did not want me around anymore. So she went back to her maternal home. Javed, leaving with me. I have heard that the President of India, Abdul Kalam Sahib, is a very kind man. And he is also very powerful. He is my last hope. I know he will help me for sure. Please, can I meet him for two minutes right now? I am sure he will help me. I am blind . . . I took two days looking for this house . . . I am thankful to Allah that I found the house today because I must go back to my village tonight.'

This man bore great sorrow in his heart and yet, through all his troubles, he did not forget to thank the Almighty for helping him find his destination in time. I really wanted to help the poor man. But Dr Kalam had gone on a tour to Chennai that day. The guard had been trying to convey this to the man when I had turned up. But the old man was president. So I asked him, 'What do you want from the President?'

His reply surprised me. It was much simpler than what I had assumed.

'I want to go back and start my own business. I have been told that many people are becoming very fat these days. I think all of them will want to measure their weight every day. My little Javed has enough education to read numbers now. I was going to ask President Sahib to give me a grant so that I can buy a weighing machine. Then we can start a business and run it together after his school. We can set the weighing machine at a local theatre near my village and the people can measure their weight there. We will make a special chart for our regular customers to help them find if they are getting thinner or not. I asked everyone I knew for some money so I could buy a weighing machine but nobody helped me. Finally, when Javed learnt about President Kalam we had some hope. Can you talk to him about this?'

Stories like this invoke to a weird mixture of guilt and gratitude in me—gratitude because we are lucky enough to be able-bodied, lucky enough to have the capability to earn our own livelihood; and guilty because we have made a society in which a blind old man has to travel far away from his home with his young grandson, just to ask for a paltry sum of money. There was no way I could arrange a meeting with Dr Kalam that day. But I wanted to help him. I did not know how much a weighing machine would cost. But I guessed it would be something around a thousand rupees. So I took out two 500-rupee notes and handed them to him. 'You can start your business now, good luck.'

He was surprised and overjoyed. He said, 'Tell the President that I knew I would not be disappointed at his doorstep. And yes, Javed will come back someday and return this money when we have enough earnings.' He turned around, happily rolling the notes into small cylinders. I went inside the gate and asked the guards to give them some water and food before they left.

The day proceeded lazily as there was little work to do. The mixed emotions that the old man had left me with still occupied a part of my thoughts.

Dr Kalam returned from Chennai in the evening. He had a habit of visiting my office after returning from a trip and chatting with me before retiring to his room. He told me a bit about his Chennai experience, and the only thing I told him about was the old man, his grandson and his business plan. He was touched by the faith that the old man had in him. He said, 'You did the right thing in helping him. I am sure Javed will come back one day. He will find you and tell you the story of his success and how you started it all. It's a great opportunity—being able to transform someone's hopes into reality. It is a story that you will always remember.'

I went back home after this conversation and got busy with other things, and life went on as usual.

Next day was a Sunday so I did not go to Dr Kalam's house and instead spent time with some of my IIM friends in Gurgaon.

On Monday, when I reached work at my usual time, refreshed after the weekend, I saw an envelope sitting on my desk. I opened it—it had a single 1000-rupee note. I did not understand what it was doing there. So I went downstairs to meet Mr Sheridon, who was Dr Kalam's private secretary and longtime aide. He was in charge of managing his finances. I asked him about the money on my desk. He just replied, 'I don't know. Boss asked me to give it to you.'

I made my way towards Dr Kalam's bedroom, which was across the upstairs library. He had almost finished his breakfast by then. I asked him boldly about the money.

He said, 'This money is for that man you helped.'

I was not at all comfortable with this. I protested, 'But you cannot reimburse me for the help that I extended.'

'But he came looking for me. I was responsible for helping him. Unfortunately, I was not there that time,' he explained.

'And fortunately I was there. So I got the chance to help him! Are you are trying to take away my *punya*!'[1] I replied jokingly.

He said, 'Look, good deeds are done by extending compassion and empathy and not by extending money. Money is actually the easiest thing to give, but it is difficult to share emotions. You will have the full punya! But I don't want you to lose money for this because you have a student loan to take care of. I can afford it—I get a good pension.'

I still did not agree to take the money.

---

[1] 'Punya' means 'positive karma' in Hindi.

After a few minutes of debating we decided to donate the 1000 rupees for a cause that I would choose and that way we could share the punya equally.

In two days, the 1000 rupees were given to a child in Connaught Place in Delhi—a child who wanted to upgrade his shoe-shining kit. His name was Hanumant and he was from Farrukhabad in Uttar Pradesh. He operated a shoe-repairing business after school, running around with a portable kit, often in his school uniform. He bought an entirely new kit with the money and increased his income. In the third or fourth meeting, he brought some old shoe-polishing friends of his, and soon we had a little group which would meet on one Sunday a month at Keventers in Connaught Place.

Until 2015, I was in touch with this kid who had received his business investment from the eleventh President of India, though the child never knew this. He had changed his business and started selling clothes in the Janpath market near Connaught Place. One day I told Hanumant and his friends, 'I will talk to Kalam Sahib and take you all to meet him.'

The kids were first confused and then delighted. 'We will see the big bungalow from inside!' one of them exclaimed. Hanumant, more thoughtful, asked, 'What gift should I give the President?'

I had no answer. They all said they would wait for the moment.

If you look around, you'll notice many such children on the roads, wooing you into giving them a chance to make your footwear look better. Quite often these little kids who are willing to shine our shoes with their small hands are ignored in the shadows are cast by the glittering lights of the posh markets around them. Dr Kalam and I often talked about these kids and about the discrimination they faced.

On 27 July 2015, while boarding a flight to Guwahati, once again we got into a discussion about the group of shoe-polishing kids. He said, 'Tell me, what can I do for them? I would love to meet them next week. Bring them home. I'll spend time with them.'

I told him, 'They'll be overjoyed to meet you!'

That meeting never happened.

And yes, as for me, I am still waiting for Javed to come and tell me his success story. I'm sure I'll hear from him one day.

31

From Missile Man to Smile Man!

In the January of 2015, an hour after noon, 30,000 villagers assembled in a large ground in the western-Indian lands of Loni in Maharashtra. Loni is about 150 kilometres north of Pune, near the holy city of Shirdi, famous for the holy saint, Sai Baba. The day was quite sunny and windless, and the huge crowd was getting increasingly uncomfortable in the stifling heat. They had gathered there to see the Missile Man of India. Dr Kalam was visiting the area on the occasion of the 50th anniversary of the Pravaranagar Rural Education Society, which had been established by Padmashri Dr Vithalrao Vikhe Patil, a renowned leader known for bringing in several agricultural reforms and the founder of the first major cooperative sugar factory in India. The movement started by Dr Patil had had spread its wings since its inception, and had gone on to establish medical and engineering colleges, hospitals, schools, training centres, banks and many other institutions. It was now being managed by his grandson, Dr Ashok Patil, who was a friend of Dr Kalam's.

Behind the makeshift stage, there were about fifty young performers who were getting ready, putting on make-up and listening to final instructions from their teachers. Three performances were planned for the event, all to be done by the children of that area. The first two were traditional dances, while the last one was a fusion dance on a patriotic song that involved a much larger troupe. We reached the function late because our flight was delayed and then we had to attend a meeting with some local people. The pilots had warned us beforehand that we had to land in Mumbai by 4.30 p.m. But after this event there was another lunch that had to be attended. So yet again we were in a time-crunch. When Dr Kalam reached the dais, we found that we hardly had sixty minutes with us. The function started off with a long but heart-warming welcome note by Dr Ashok Patil, after which there was a small award ceremony. And then the performers took the stage. Concerned about the time, we requested Dr Patil to get Dr Kalam's address started as soon as possible because he would need at least twenty-five to thirty minutes to go through all his points. Dr Patil was a man of wonderful manners, and he took this request so seriously that he cancelled the last performance. The organizers decided that the performance would be conducted only after Dr Kalam had departed for lunch.

It was a drastic step, but it saved us some ten minutes. After the second performance, when Dr Kalam began walking towards the podium, I went up to him to pin the collar mic on him and told him that the third performance had been cancelled to save time, so he need not worry about keeping his speech short. He looked at me and asked, 'And what about the performers?' I told him that they would perform after he had left. He replied, 'Ah! Do you think that will work?' He was right. I knew that once he left, the majority of the crowd would leave as well.

By the time Dr Kalam stepped away from the podium amidst a roaring applause from 30,000 people, the cancelled performance had been forgotten by all but one person. We finished the event and quickly went to the nearby office building where a wonderful vegetarian lunch had been served for Dr Kalam and the others. His favourite items— bhindi, onion ring pakoras and yogurt—had been served. We were in the middle of a conversation at the lunch table when Dr Kalam suddenly turned to Dr Ashok Patil and said, 'I have a request. Let us hasten the lunch and save some time. Then can you please ask the children from the third performance to come here? They must be feeling sad, I am sure. I want to meet them and console them.' About ten people were present at the lunch and everyone paused for a moment, awed by Dr Kalam's sensitivity.

In five minutes about fifteen to twenty young children, in full make-up and colourful costumes, gathered outside the room. Dr Kalam was right. They were quite disappointed and the younger ones were crying—the mascara that the little girls had put in their eyes had been washed away by their tears. As soon as they saw Dr Kalam coming towards them, some of them got very emotional and started crying all over again. These little children had practised for months in front of his portrait to motivate themselves. Now their disappointment changed to utter joy. Dr Kalam cut down on his lunch to ensure that he could spend more than the five minutes he had promised with them. He asked the children their names and posed for many photographs with them. Finally as he was leaving Dr Ashok Patil remarked, 'These children got luckier by not performing today because they got to spend all that time with you directly.'

The children laughed heartily. We were all touched by the compassion of the great Missile Man or, should I say, the 'Smile Man'?

32

The Appropriate Inheritance

On the night of 23 July 2015, I was flying back to Delhi from Ahmedabad. I had spent about a week in Gujarat for some work. From 24 to 26 July Dr Kalam and I were supposed to sit in the office and spend the weekend finalizing lectures and projects for the programme at IIM Shillong. This programmme was supposed to be held on 27 and 28 July 2015. Dr Kalam was always aware of my exact itinerary because we used to be in contact over our mobile phones whenever I was not in Delhi.

On 23rd July I landed at about 9 p.m. and left for Dr Kalam's house where I was going to stay that night. As soon as I entered my room on the first floor of his house, I got a call from him.

He asked me, 'You funny fellow! Have you reached?' When I said 'yes' he immediately asked me to meet him.

As soon as I walked into his reading room, he showed me an email that he had received from the students of Professor N. Balakrishnan, whom we used to address as Balki. Professor

Balki, who worked at the Indian Institute of Science, Bangalore, was a longtime associate of Dr Kalam's. They had worked together in the aerospace sector. Dr Balki played a very crucial role in developing India's first super computer. Dr Balki was retiring, so his students wanted to make a video collage in his honour with messages from all the people he had worked with. The students wanted Dr Kalam to send a video message for this collage. They wanted to show these videos to their professor at a small event on 25 July.

It was already 11 p.m. so I said that we could get this done professionally the next morning. He looked at me, surprised. 'But they want the message today. We must send it by today itself. They are doing something for their teacher and we should help them. Balki is a good fellow!'

There was only one alternative left—to use my mobile phone to shoot this video. We went to the office room and together we engineered a makeshift tripod with books to keep the phone steady. Dr Kalam sat down on a chair while I adjusted the camera. He said, 'See which pose looks better. It should be a good video!'

'Sure! Let's try that,' I replied enthusiastically.

Then he proceeded to change postures each time I clicked the camera and we ended up taking half a dozen different pictures. Finally he chose the posture that looked best and I began recording a five-minute extempore message.

When the message was recorded, I told him that I would process and send off the video in about half an hour. He said he would wait with me. Soon we got drawn into another conversation.

'Three days ago, on the 20th, I was in Dindigul, where I met my old professor, who is ninety plus years old—Professor Ladislaus Chinnadurai . . . He taught me physics. He was so happy to see me. I thanked him and tears rolled down his cheeks. He told everyone, "Even after sixty years, Kalam remembered me and my teaching." He gave me a certificate for being a good student. I felt blessed. You know what gift I gave him?'

'What?' I stopped my work and asked curiously. Ten per cent of the video had been uploaded by then.

Tapping one finger softly on the table, he said, 'I gave him our book, *Reignited*. I told him that I had written this book with a young fellow who was my student at IIM. Like I was your student, he is my student. He went through the book quickly, reading a page or two, and said that it seemed like a good book. He will read it completely and give us marks out of a hundred. I think we will get good marks from my teacher. He seemed happy with whatever little he read. Then you will also get a good certificate from my teacher.'

We both laughed.

About twenty per cent of the upload was completed.

'I think these fellows who asked us to make this video are basically good students. They are doing fantastic work for their retiring professor. Students and youth should take care of their teachers . . . and also of their parents. I am worried that the young are forgetting their teachers and parents as they rise in life.'

Thirty per cent of the upload was done.

Then he immediately corrected himself, 'Not everyone does this but some fellows are there who ignore the people who've sacrificed their lives to make them who they are. You be a good fellow and don't ignore your parents and teachers ever in your life—even when they are not here any more. I still derive so much from my parents and from all my teachers though they left this world many decades ago . . .'

I kept listening to him while working on the video. The Internet was running slowly and it was taking a long time to upload just a 300 MB file. He continued.

'Parents also need to change themselves. Children need time and attention from their parents, much more than they need resources and commodities. People amass wealth all through their lives. They cross all limits of hoarding—this hunger for wealth takes them to the brink of madness. It is as if they are drinking sea water to quench their thirst—the more they drink the thirstier they feel. Their never-ending struggle is like a deer running after a mirage—it makes them sick, makes them sad, and even kills them. Often they do not do this amassing just for themselves; they do it for their next generation, and sometimes for even more than just one generation. To create a bequest of wealth for their children, they forget to create the bridges of compassion and love.'

'But does this make their children happier? Does it even make them grateful to their parents? I doubt . . .' I said as the upload crossed fifty per cent.

'If it had worked then the sons of the richest people would not have started fighting after their deaths. Wealth, which they leave behind, only yields fear, jealousy and squabbles. I believe one should never create the smallest of bequests through wealth.'

'But then what should they give their children?' I asked.

Sixty per cent upload completed.

He summed it up, 'My father used to say that there is only one source of light and people just act as the holes in the lamp shade. We should be ready to give away whatever we get for ourselves. And even seven decades later my father's words still ring true. Whatever a person gets in life should be used up for good causes. The fruits of these good actions will become the inheritance for the next generations. One should leave behind a legacy of love and the wealth of wisdom because sharing love and wisdom never creates any boundaries.' He added further, just to clarify his point, 'Wealth is a very inappropriate thing to inherit.'

Ninety per cent upload completed.

'So the best thing to leave behind is wisdom and not wealth. Is that right?' I asked.

'Yes, that way one knows that there will be peace after him and love will blossom amongst those he has left behind.'

'True. That is how one should take leave,' I added.

'Yes. And goodbyes should be short, really short. Short goodbyes create lasting memories. The best moment to go is when one is standing tall, wearing shoes at work, and doing something one loves to do. That is a classic exit. Imagine a great show. As soon as it is over, the curtains should come down, without delays. That way the performers will only be remembered for the great show that they executed.'

A beep came from the computer. Hundred per cent upload completed.

'Kya baat hai! Bohot achha!' (Wow! Very good!) he exclaimed happily. Sometimes he would use a bit of Hindi to appreciate my work; this meant that he was very happy with the results and that he wanted to ease the stress. I would also occasionally pick some select words from Tamil to converse with him—his Hindi and my Tamil never failed to make others laugh.

He got up saying, 'Go and sleep. Tomorrow we will work on the IIM Shillong lectures; they are very important. I want to especially work on the Creating a Liveable Planet Earth lecture; this topic is very critical in these times. I want the young fellows to take some actions after hearing my lecture.'

Dr Kalam lived his beliefs, in life and in death.

Exactly four days later, on 27 July, when he said his last goodbye, it was short—really, really short—lasting for just a few seconds. He was standing tall on a podium doing exactly what he loved—teaching. He fell down only once and then I took off his shoes. In his final performance he was a teacher who was trying to tell his students to forget their boundaries and their divisions and save the planet as one. Then the curtains fell.

Talented people get to choose where and how they live, how much wealth they live with, but only noble souls get to choose how they depart and what love they carry with them when they depart.

On the 28th, when his own bequest was counted, it mostly comprised thousands of books, a few articles of clothing, a very modest bank balance and . . . an insurmountable love for people, overwhelming wisdom and impeccable integrity.

I Will Come Back And Vote

On 4 December 2013, the Delhi Assembly elections were held after a chaotic campaign where three parties were prominent—BJP, Congress and the newly formed Aam Admi Party (AAP). As always, Dr Kalam was religious about his right to vote, and he went to the nearest polling station early in the morning. While he was waiting for his turn, the Electronic Voting Machine (EVM) suddenly stopped working and the voting had to be halted. Seeing the former President standing in the queue, the officers there panicked and hurried to set the machine right. Dr Kalam calmly waited with the rest of the people. After several minutes his staff suggested that he return home. But before leaving the polling booth he told the officers, 'Whenever the EVM starts working, I will come back and vote.'

Sure enough, he went back to the polling booth again an hour later and cast his vote.

In 2009, the Centre for Environment Education had conducted a nationwide polling across 2 lakh schools, where children could vote for their 'Bharat ka Paryavaran Ambassador'. The children of India almost unanimously elected Dr Kalam as their environment ambassador. Dr Kalam took this responsibility very seriously and from then on he made sure he talked more about environmental issues in his speeches.

33

Humility Is the Path to Greatness

Dr Kalam was best known for his humility. In fact, it was perhaps this particular trait that separated him from the rest of the successful scientists and politicians. His humility was not manufactured; it was innate and shone through in his daily life. His humility was evident when he wiped his table himself post lunch, when he wore the simplest of clothing, and when he tidied his old articles and books himself. He was happiest when he was meeting ordinary citizens.

In 2012, Dr Kalam visited a function where some bureaucrats, ministers and other senior officers were in attendance. I was with him. It was a reasonably well-organized function, but since many civil-service officers were present, very rigid and clear lines of hierarchies were evident.

When Dr Kalam came up to the dais he suddenly stopped. He spotted that the chairs on the dais were of different shapes and sizes. The chair that was placed for him in the centre of the stage was the tallest and the most majestic. He requested that his special chair be replaced with an ordinary one. This left the other senior officers and ministers completely bemused. When another associate from our office and I started to pull the chair away, the other officers rushed forward, not to help us, but to look for junior officers who could do the job for us. Soon two junior officers joined us and we successfully replaced the chair. Dr Kalam and I smiled at this stark discrimination.

On our way back I mentioned the incident again to him. He smiled. 'Yes! I noticed them spending too much energy looking for someone else to finish such a simple task. Leaders should set better examples. Only then can we change the next generation of officers. The junior fellows will do exactly what the senior fellows are showing them now.'

He continued, 'In my days I had some wonderful examples—that was how my bosses became my gurus as well. Dr V.S. Arunachalam was heading DRDO when we were preparing for the Agni launch in 1989. He was my boss. We were at the Chandipur range in Odisha at that time. A day before the launch we had a meeting with the launch authorization board which, as one would expect, was an opportunity for many debates, discussions, arguments and counter-arguments. All of us were determined to complete the project successfully, which would propel India many steps up the ladder in missile technology. Our tireless planning and evaluation went right up to 2 a.m. on the morning of the launch. After the meeting, Dr Arunachalam and I were returning to the guest house from the block house where we had conducted the meeting. It was a relatively long drive. I fell asleep in the car. None of the road-bumps and curves on the path could wake me up. When we reached the guest house Dr Arunachalam gently tapped me, and I found that my head was on his shoulder. I felt very embarrassed; after all he was my boss. I had probably kept my head on his shoulder all through the journey and he didn't want to disturb me. I wonder, in today's bureaucracy, will any boss allow such a thing to happen? Of course Dr Arunachalam was more a friend than a boss. Hierarchies were surpassed by personal friendships; this was the culture, power gaps meant little to us.'

It was a moving story—indeed a lesson in today's time. I could see how such stalwarts had shaped Dr Kalam into the icon he was. I too had a story to share with him on this topic.

'Sir, you know, I recently read a story about George Washington, the first President of the United States and their founding father. When the US war of independence was going on in the 1770s, George Washington was leading the Americans against the British forces. Back then, because of the lack of newspapers, cameras or televisions, few people recognized George Washington by face, despite him being a national leader. One day, when he was passing by with a small number of guards, he saw a couple of soldiers struggling to push a cart across a small stream. The cart was heavy and it kept rolling back. Behind them was a major, who was shouting at them from a distance to push harder. When George Washington saw this, he got down from his horse and walked up to the major, who failed to recognize him. He asked the major why he was only telling the soldiers what to do and not helping them himself. The major replied, "Because I am a major. I cannot push the cart with the soldiers." George Washington went up to the struggling soldiers and started pushing the cart with them. With the extra help, the cart finally crossed the stream. Returning to the major, Washington remarked, "Next time you need someone to help your soldiers push the cart, ask for the commander-in-chief." It was then that the major and his soldiers realized who had really helped them. This commander-in-chief won the war of independence within two years and against a much stronger Britain.'

My story ended.

Dr Kalam concluded, 'This is what generals and bosses should be like. The commander-in-chief has to be like the legendary tree—the taller it grows the more it bends towards its roots. Through humility and compassion emerges the path to greatness.'

34

The Warrior of Love

This is the tale of how two heroes met—one, of course, was Dr Kalam, my guru, and the other was a young friend of mine, Raghu, lesser known but nevertheless a man of determination and unrelenting joy, evident from his smiles.

Who was Raghu?

In 2010, Raghu, all of twenty-six then, had already earned the title 'Warrior of Love' because of his untiring service. He was a young man whose skin was tanned by the long hours spent under the sun, with pleasantly radiant eyes and shining teeth which were always visible because of his smile. Raghu had a golden heart which had been moulded by the fires of adversity. When he was only a year old, he was struck by polio, which took away the mobility from his legs. So he learnt to walk on his hands. Even though he was poor he went out of his way to help others. Most people would have buckled under the strain of adversities that Raghu had experienced in his life. At the age of twenty, Raghu left his village with merely

300 rupees in his pocket but with a mission to help the society.

Raghu used to move around in a three-wheeled motorcycle, which had been donated to him by a local NGO. The resilient and ever-smiling Raghu was an ambassador of goodwill who helped others stand tall while he himself walked around on his palms.

Raghu lived a life which can be best described as a journey of love and service. Every morning he would fight with his mother, the only family he had, to convince her to fill some two dozen tiffin boxes with home-cooked food. He called them *Pyaar nu Tiffin* (the Tiffin of Love). With these boxes of food, he would then get on his three-wheeled motorcycle and travel through streets and slums. He would pick out the needy and distribute this food to them. Pyaar nu Tiffin was free—sumptuous food garnished with love. Raghu did this every single day, whether the day was rainy, sunny or chilly. He would feed others even if his own kitchen was running low in supplies. A handful of people encouraged him and Raghu's tiffin boxes had a hundred per cent success rate. Once I had asked Raghu how he managed to make food for two dozen people daily with his limited resources. He replied, '*Srijan bhai, upar wala karata hai. Uska plan hai. Woh humein deta rahega, taki hum aage dete rahein.*' (The Almighty makes me do it. It is his plan. He gives to us so that we can pass it along.)

One of his supporters was a young social entrepreneur, Amitabh Shah. He was a graduate from Yale University who had started the NGO YUVA Unstoppable, connecting youth with socially relevant work. When YUVA turned five years old, Amitabh invited Dr Kalam for the anniversary celebrations.

This is where these two heroes met. Amitabh was careful and smart enough not to make any celebrity or industrialist sit next to Dr Kalam on the stage. The person sitting beside him was none other than Raghu himself. Throughout the function they chatted with each other and Dr Kalam asked him, 'What is your dream in life?'

Raghu replied, 'I want to see the women of India and their children smile.' Dr Kalam was so moved by this reply that he opened his speech with these very words that day. Raghu had left a deep impression in his heart. He even asked Raghu to join him while he was giving away some of the awards for social service.

Raghu's story became a part of Dr Kalam's speeches on a few occasions after that. Time moved and Raghu evolved further. He used to call me often and we would exchange motivational messages with each other.

Three years later, in January 2013, Raghu fell in love with a girl. They would go out together on the bike to distribute the tiffins. Raghu had added a new and joyful chapter to his life.

On 10 February 2013, he reluctantly took a day off from distributing the tiffin boxes so he could take his fiancée to his village to fix the wedding date in consultation with his family. On the way, the three-wheeler motorcycle was struck by a fast-moving truck. Raghu died on the spot. His fiancée, though injured, survived.

I couldn't believe that my friend, all of twenty-nine, had passed away just as he was about to begin a new phase of his life. I consoled myself with his words—it is the plan of the Almighty. I shared the news with Dr Kalam. Three years had passed since they last met but Dr Kalam remembered him clearly. He was saddened by the news and immediately inquired about his family's whereabouts. Thankfully there were many people who were ready to support his mother. But all she needed was recognition of the fact that her son had lived a worthy life.

So Dr Kalam wrote a condolence letter. It was a short letter written on the official letterhead but it carried great weight:

I am saddened to learn about the sudden demise of Raghu Makwana. Raghu's compassionate and kind work for helping the needy at his small age will always be remembered by the society. I pray to the Almighty for the departed soul and also for giving strength to his family to bear the irreparable loss.

A.P.J. Abdul Kalam

Such letters from heads of state or former heads of state are written only for celebrities, famous politicians, industrialists, that is, for men of great power and wealth. But Raghu's life, his work, his love, his compassion and his smile had earned him this respect from Dr Kalam.

Raghu was a hero, in life and in death. He was indeed the warrior of love.

35

True Religion Is Service in Oblivion

Dr Kalam and I would frequently discuss religion and spirituality. He was my spiritual teacher. This might seem unusual for a man of science, but the beauty of his spirit lay in that very fact.

Because he had the mind of a scientist, he used to test all that he found in religion on the altar of reason. And because he had the heart of a saint, his altar of reason and judgement was not merely confined to the borders of proven facts but propelled by thoughts of all that is possible. The convergence of science and spirituality often happens at the horizon of this human imagination.

He was well versed in many different scriptures, and of course, he had absorbed learnings from many great minds. Often our conversations about spirituality would create a relatively relaxed environment around us. One day in 2011, I asked him, 'Sir, what is the correct way to serve any religion?'

He gave me a beautiful response—holistic and complete with an example.

He replied, 'It was 15 May 1998. India had just conducted its five nuclear tests successfully, thus elevating its defence preparedness. The mood in the nation was one of jubilation. My team and I were returning from Pokhran, the site for the tests. Pokhran is a place situated deep in the west-Indian desert of Thar, and very little life exists there. The temperatures were soaring over fifty degrees Celsius. On our way back, meandering through the desert roads, we came across a small village, Bhadariya. On seeing the signboard, my friend Dr K.N. Rai's eyes immediately lit up. He exclaimed that he knew the place and had heard about a certain ashram there. We decided to take a small detour and visit the ashram on his request. Bhadariya was a small hamlet, and while it was not quite difficult to locate the ashram, it was difficult to believe what we saw once we reached there. It was a large place in the middle of the desert, filled with greenery.

'The head priest of the ashram, Baba Sri Bhadariya Maharaj, greeted us and asked us whether we would like to see the unique library he had created. He then took us down the staircase and into an underground chamber which led to the library. We were pleasantly surprised to find that the room was remarkably cool and was filled with more than two lakh books on different subjects, different languages and different historical periods. Some of them were even handwritten on parchments. Baba Sri Bhadariya Maharaj told us that the architectural design of the building was such that even when the temperature rose up to fifty degrees, the library would be naturally air-conditioned. He showed us books which were hundreds of years old, and told us that the ashram had conserved traditional knowledge through the ages.

'While we were reading in the library, mesmerized by its cultural wealth, he brought us huge glasses of milk. I asked him, "Baba, in the middle of this desert, where do you get such delicious, fresh milk?" He smiled and asked me to follow him. There, behind the ashram, we saw a huge cow shelter with about a thousand cows. Baba then said, "Kalam! These are all ostracized cows. People drove them away from their homes when they stopped giving milk. For them, these cows were useless. But you see, just like you, I am also a technologist." He laughed. "I have a special method of treating the stray cows and today they are all healthy, happy and producing large quantities of quality milk, some of which you have in your glass." I was amazed to see such a noble mission. I asked, "But Baba, where do you find fodder for all these animals?" Baba Sri Bhadariya Maharaj asked me to sit down on a small charpoy under the shade, and started telling me a story.

'He told me, "Kalam, years ago the people of this place were very poor and addicted to many types of intoxicants, including liquor, tobacco and other forms of local weeds. This place was barren and devoid of trees. There were a plethora of problems here like poverty, hunger, lack of healthcare and malnutrition. Water was scarce and yet poorly managed. Look at what we did then with cooperation and support from the villagers. We started a de-addiction campaign right here in the ashram, which has now spread to over seventy villages around Bhadariya. We executed a mission of greening Bhadariya and its surrounding areas with the help of local support, and planted lakhs of trees. We got tube wells dug; agriculture started in this place. We developed special ways to conserve water." Baba then passionately continued, "This ashram also provides knowledge about naturopathy and herbal medicines to the rural communities. We teach how to treat cattle. Medicines for the cattle are prepared with a special technology using locally available herbs." He finally told me, "You know, Kalam, the villagers are so happy about all this that they provide fodder for these cows. Of course, when the cows start giving milk I give away the milk and butter free of cost to the needy and to the travellers passing through this place. Like yourself, Kalam!" He laughed as he said that and asked me whether I wanted a refill, which I was happy to accept. "One final question, Baba. Where does all this knowledge about local herbs, cow-rehabilitation techniques and other things that you are doing come from?" Baba Bhadariya's eyes twinkled as he smilingly pointed to the underground library. "From there!"'

Dr Kalam paused for a moment before continuing. 'So the answer to your question lies in the life of this Baba. I believe, real service to religion is in serving the remotest of villages. True servants of religion will choose to move away from urban comforts and head to unknown places, in oblivion, where people face unimaginable difficulties. That is how religious service can truly enrich the heart. Bhadariya may be a small place in the middle of the Thar Desert, but it can still offer a great lesson to the world.'

Who Is Your Favourite Character from the Mahabharata?

The Mahabharata was one of our favourite points of discussion.

One day, while talking about the epic, I asked him, 'Who is your favourite character?'

Without a pause he replied, 'Vidur.'

I was surprised. 'Vidur did not fight the war. He was not even a king. What makes him your favourite?'

Dr Kalam explained, 'Vidur stood for Dharma. He was the most intelligent person in the epic. He knew sacrifice, as he did not even stake a claim to the throne and gave it away to his brother. He knew courage, as he protested against Draupadi's humiliation. He maintained wisdom and patience even in the wake of war and destruction. He is the embodiment of conscience in the Mahabharata. His actions are clear and follow dharma. So he is my favourite.'

36

I Want to Hear Him Speak
Beautifully Again . . .

In May 2014, Dr Kalam, Sheridon and I visited the beautiful country of Scotland in the northern part of the United Kingdom. We stayed in the capital city of Edinburgh (pronounced Edinborough). Despite being the capital, it is a sparsely populated city with less than five lakh people. We were there because Dr Kalam was receiving an honorary doctorate from the famous University of Edinburgh. He was the first Indian to be bestowed with this honour. The University of Edinburgh, founded in 1582, is the alma mater of some of the best-known human minds, including Charles Darwin, Thomas Bayes Maxwell, Sir Walter Scott and Sir Arthur Conan Doyle. It has an association with over twenty Nobel Laureates.

Edinburgh itself is a marvel, rated amongst the best cities in the world. All the buildings have a rustic feel to them; the major junctions and crossways boast of beautiful statues and foundations, and large gardens adorn the city.

We stayed at the historic Hotel Waldorf Astoria Edinburgh—The Caledonian. Dr Kalam's room overlooked the Edinburgh Castle which was positioned on the famous Castle Rock.

As usual, there were a number of visits planned to the laboratories of the university. One of the visits was to the Anne Rowling Regenerative Neurology Clinic. The laboratory is largely funded by J.K. Rowling, the creator of the famous Harry Potter series, in memory of her mother, Anne, who had lost her life battling brain degeneration. There we met Professor Siddharthan Chandran, who had migrated from India and was heading the centre. He showed us all the work that was being conducted in this small but cutting-edge laboratory. We were all particularly impressed with the work on early detection of mental and neural disorders. Professor Chandran showed us his work deploying technology typically used by eye-care professionals.

As we were about to end our hour-long tour inside the laboratory we came across one last researcher—a young lady from England. She was working on a technology to regenerate speech. Her project was aimed at those people who were suffering from slow brain degeneration and who were likely to lose their voice in a few years. This condition is called dysarthria. And the innovative project that was being developed to fix it is called Voice Banking. Through this method, a person who is about to lose his or her voice can speak into a device and store it. The device can store a huge repository of words. Once the disease sets in, and the person loses his or her voice, this voice bank becomes the tool through which they can communicate. When the voiceless person types some words on a keyboard the device says those words out loud in his or her voice. The lead researcher said, 'In this way the world can hear them in their original voice.'

We were all very impressed. But Dr Kalam had a follow-up question, 'But what if the person is already unable to speak much?'

'I'm afraid we can operate only when we can actually record a person's voice, and that too thousands of words,' said the researcher.

'Okay, what if some existing speeches are supplied—say, someone's speech that is recorded in the past?' Dr Kalam probed further.

This time Professor Chandran replied, 'Oh! We have not thought of this yet. But if we can isolate the words from the past recordings, and map them, then it should be possible. Once our ongoing experiment gets over in a year, we can surely try that too.'

'Please do let me know next year. I am keen to find out,' Dr Kalam insisted.

We moved on. I asked him in the car, 'You seemed most interested in this Voice Bank.'

'You know why?'

'I don't know.'

'Because I have a friend, a wonderful man whom I respect a lot. He was a great orator once but now he has a lot of difficulty in speaking fluently. I want to hear him speak beautifully again. You know who he is?'

And before I could think of a reply, he answered his own question. 'Vajpayeeji.'

'We should definitely check with them next year, to see whether they can construct a Voice Bank using old speeches. I will propose this solution to Vajpayeeji's folks if these scientists give the green signal. I wish I could give him this gift on his birthday next year.'

'That will be a wonderful Christmas present from Edinburgh,' I replied, recalling that Vajpayeeji's birthday coincided with Christmas.

'Yes.' We both smiled. It was touching to see his concern and compassion for his 'old friend', whom he dearly respected. Incidentally, Vajpayeeji used to live just 30 metres away from Dr Kalam's house.

This idea had remained in his mind ever since. On 25 December 2014, when Dr Kalam met Vajpayeeji for the latter's ninety-first birthday, he asked me to post this message on his social media:

Just arrived home after meeting Shri Atal Bihari Vajpayeeji at his residence in New Delhi. I greeted him on his birthday and also congratulated him for being awarded the much deserved Bharat Ratna.

I told him, 'Vajpayeeji, I have had the privilege of working with you for more than five years as the Principal Scientific Advisor to the Government and then as the President of India while you were the Prime Minister. I learnt so much from you. I learnt from your experience in building India as a great and strong nation. When we decided to make it a Nuclear Weapon State we agreed to a unilateral no first-use policy. I admire how you as a Prime Minister embarked on the mission of unifying the minds and hearts of a billion strong nation.'

With those words I greeted the stalwart leader and wished him a long life.

When this message was posted, Dr Kalam commented, 'Maybe next year I will have a wonderful gift for him.' This gift remained an unfulfilled dream of Dr Kalam's.

37

The External Teacher

In 1982, a nineteen-year-old man from Virudhanagar in Tamil Nadu joined the Army as a sepoy. His name was V. Kathiresan. Soon he was deputed to DRDL in Hyderabad to be the driver of a senior scientist—Dr A.P.J. Abdul Kalam.

A few days into his job, when he was driving his master around, the latter inquired, 'Till which level have you studied, Kathiresan?'

'I failed the tenth standard. I failed in English.' The young man was unapologetic about his failure in this foreign language.

'Oh! You must definitely pass the tenth standard. And you must do well in English,' said his fifty-year-old youthful boss, throwing him a challenge. Seeing the young driver's hesitation, his boss assured, 'I will help you.'

Soon Kathiresan and Dr Kalam established a student-mentor relationship. Their goal was small—to pass Class 10 and do well particularly in English. Dr Kalam, after completing his daily schedule at DRDO, would teach

Kathiresan some basics in English, especially grammar. Within a year, Kathiresan passed the exam.

However, Dr Kalam had higher goals for him. He just chose to convey the goals one step at a time. After all, he would one day be famously known for his statement, 'Small aim is a crime.'

'Now you should also complete the 12th grade.' Dr Kalam gave young Kathiresan a new target. To give confidence to the young driver, he decided to pay the exam fees and buy him the requisite books. To motivate him further, Dr Kalam set a race between the two—post work they would both read their own books. The master read from his library and the driver from his syllabus. Whoever read more, won. Finally, young Kathiresan secured 51.4 per cent in his Class 12 exams, all because of the confidence and support he got from his master. He was elated. But Dr Kalam wasn't done.

'You should study computer science. Do a B.Sc.' The visionary Dr Kalam knew that computers were going to shape the world one day and he also knew that this young man could make a wonderful career out of it. But this time they had to reach a compromise. Kathiresan's interest was in humanities. So they settled for him completing his Bachelors in Arts. Now the scientist taught his driver-cum-student the history of the world, particularly the two World Wars. Kathiresan secured 51 per cent in his exams. His family was overjoyed. Kathiresan thought he had achieved enough.

His master was still not satisfied. He wanted to push his student further. 'You should get a postgraduate degree now. I think you should pursue political science.' Kathiresan was happy with the faith that his master had in him but he felt intimidated by the challenge. The master himself had just a bachelor's degree in technology. With a master's, the driver would have a degree higher than that of his boss! Great teachers always want their students to achieve more than they themselves achieve in their lifetime. Dr Kalam was an exemplary teacher, no doubt. But Kathiresan had too many hurdles in his path. On one occasion he was about to miss an exam when Dr Kalam helped him by buying him an air ticket so his pupil would not miss his postgraduate exams in Chennai.

Within a decade of joining Dr Kalam's office as a driver, Kathiresan had passed the tenth, twelfth, B.A, MA, B.Ed. and M.Ed exams.

In 1992, Kathiresan had to return to his position in the Army, so he parted ways with his master. But in 1998, he took a voluntary retirement so that he could continue with his educational journey which had now become a passion for him. He registered for a PhD in Manonmaniam Sundaranar University and finished the course in 2001. Thereafter, he joined the Education Department of Tamil Nadu Government and served for a number of years. In 2010, he became an assistant professor at the Government Arts College in Tirunelveli.

Both the driver-student and the master-teacher duo gave each other something to be proud of, something to tell stories about.

When Dr Kalam was narrating this story, praising Kathiresan, someone asked him, 'What spark did you see in him?'

'I used to notice that he always read books, newspapers and journals of substance in his free time . . . and he would read meticulously. I was struck by his dedication. I asked him what made him read so much during his leisure time. He said that he had a son and a daughter and they would ask him a lot of questions. That made him study so that he could answer their questions to the best of his abilities. I was impressed by his spirit, so I told him to study formally through the distance-education mode. He took that as a challenge and kept on studying.'

And when someone from the crowd asked what message the youth should derive from the life of Kathiresan, Dr Kalam replied, 'With commitment and dedication he has acquired the right skills in his leisure time and that has helped him progress in his career and upgrade his livelihood. The message is that it doesn't matter who you are. If you have a vision and the determination to achieve that vision, then you will certainly succeed. Can you all repeat this with me?'

Dreams transform into thoughts and
Thoughts result in action

The crowd repeated each word he said respectfully and confidently; the air reverberated with the strength of the echo.

After Dr Kalam passed away, when Kathiresan was preparing to leave for Rameswaram to pay his last respects he said, 'I have one regret—not having learnt computers.'

* * *

'There are half a dozen computers in this building. Why don't you learn to operate them, instead of watching TV all the time?'

Chellapa, a soldier from the Indian Army who had been assigned to the former President of India, was lying flat on a couch and flipping through channels on the TV after completing his daily chores. Recognizing Dr Kalam's voice, he jumped off the couch. While one foot landed on the right slipper the other slipped on the left slipper, which skidded under the couch. Standing straight, he exclaimed, 'Sir!' He wondered if he should reach out for the remote and shut the TV.

'Till what class have you studied, Chellapa?' Dr Kalam repeated the question that he often asked those who worked with him.

'Sir, I am a tenth pass, sir,' replied Chellapa.

'Oh. You must then complete your twelfth. It is not that difficult. And also study computers; they will be useful to you. I will designate one of the office computers so that you can learn on it, after office hours.' Dr Kalam would insist on computer literacy over and over again.

'Replace some TV time with study time.' With those words he left the sitting room.

Chellapa used to serve Dr Kalam his food. Whenever Dr Kalam met him after that, he would ask, 'Are you taking the twelfth exams?' or 'Are you learning how to work on the computer?' He would quickly add, 'Let me know if you need any help with the exams.'

Chellapa knew that he was under constant watch. After some hesitation he too embarked on the same journey that Kathiresan had set out on almost three decades ago.

Today, Chellapa, who managed Dr Kalam's house till his master's last day, has a bachelor's degree, and is an expert on computer applications.

38

The Last Eight Hours—A Teacher Forever

27 July 2015

The slightly overcast day began with hectic travelling, without any signs of the ominous and life-changing end it had in store for us.

Our journey from Delhi to Shillong was broken into two parts. First, we were to fly to Guwahati, have lunch at the Guwahati Airport and then travel further to Shillong via road. Dr Kalam was scheduled to conduct a class on Creating a Liveable Planet Earth that evening and his class was supposed to be followed by student presentations. As always, he wanted me to conduct fifteen minutes of the lecture. On that fateful day, we reached the airport by noon. We were allotted seat numbers 1-A (his) and 1-C (mine). Dr Kalam was wearing a dark-grey-coloured 'Kalam suit', a typical bandhgala. He used to wear such bandhgalas regardless of the weather. It was a relatively new suit. I started off by complimenting him, 'Nice colour!' We had a long two and a half hours of flying in the turbulent monsoon weather. I hate turbulence, but he had mastered his fear. Whenever he would see me go cold on a jerky flight he would just pull down the window shutter and reassure me saying, 'Now you won't see any fear!'

We were talking about the scheduled lecture when suddenly he noticed a bright, dancing spot of light on the plane wall in front of us—something was reflecting the sunlight and creating these patterns of light on the wall. He asked me, 'Do you know what is reflecting this?' First I thought it was his wrist watch, and then I guessed it was his pen. Both the guesses were wrong. He had a black bag, which he always carried with him as hand baggage. He never stowed that bag in the overhead bin while travelling in planes; he'd rather keep it close to himself. He pointed at the shiny zipper of this bag and said, 'From this. It is really shiny, isn't it? Why don't you put it on Twitter and see how many of our fellows can guess it?'

The plane landed in Guwahati sometime after 2 p.m. As always I asked him to go ahead while I picked up his handbag after him. The bag looked stuffed and was unusually heavy. I asked him, 'What are you carrying? Seems like construction material!'

He replied, 'Oh, that is for the journey. It has four books that I am reading these days. I thought during this twelve-hour back-and-forth journey I could finish some reading.'

Srijan Pal Singh

It was amazing that an eighty-three-year-old man, who had already made his mark in the world, was still hungry for knowledge. But then wisdom usually comes to those who have the kind of childlike curiosity that Dr Kalam did.

We proceeded for lunch at the airport lounge, in a modest room decorated with some old artefacts.

Mr Sharma, PA to Dr Kalam, was accompanying us on the trip to ensure that all the documents were taken care of and to make sure that we adhered to our timelines. He was a talented singer and actor, and throughout the lunch Dr Kalam kept urging him to mimic different people.

Once lunch was over we embarked on the second leg of our journey. That was another two and a half hours of driving to IIM Shillong. During the five hours of this two-pronged journey we talked, discussed and debated. That journey was one of the longest that we had taken together in the last six years. Like the other trips, this one was also turning out to be as special. Three discussions in particular that day will remain as special memories of our final trip.

First, Dr Kalam was tremendously worried about the attacks in Punjab. On the morning of 27 July, three gunmen dressed in army uniforms had opened fire on a bus and had attacked a police station in the Gurdaspur district of Punjab. The attack had resulted in the death of three civilians and four policemen, including a superintendent of police. The loss of innocent lives had filled him with sorrow. The lecture that we were going to deliver that day at IIM Shillong was on the topic Creating a Liveable Planet Earth. He related the Punjab attacks to the lecture topic and said, 'It seems that man-made forces are as big a threat to the habitability of earth as is pollution.' We surmised that if this trend of violence, pollution and reckless human behaviour continued then we would be forced to leave this earth soon. 'Thirty years, at this rate, maybe,' he said. 'You young fellows must do something about it . . . it is going to be your world in the future.'

Our second discussion was mostly about national politics. For the past two days, Dr Kalam had been worried about the Parliament—the supreme institution of democracy—becoming dysfunctional. He said, 'I have seen two different governments during my tenure as President and many more after that. But this disruption just keeps happening, irrespective of the ruling government. This is not right. I really need to find out a way to ensure that the Parliament starts working on developmental politics now.'

He then asked me to prepare a surprise assignment for the students at IIM Shillong, which he would give them only at the end of the lecture. He wanted the students to suggest three innovative ways to make the Parliament more productive and functional.

--- ✳ ---

The Surprise Assignment for the IIM Shillong Students

Dear friends, as I conclude today's lecture let me give you a small assignment on a very important issue which affects the nation. As you might have read in the news, the Parliament in Delhi is stalled for the whole of this session over various issues and deadlocks. Of course, a non-functioning Parliament hampers national development and growth.

I have been the President of India from 2002 to 2007 and in that time I saw two different governments. Under both of them, there were many issues where the Parliament did not function for many days, leading to loss to the nation.

I want three of you to volunteer to come up here tomorrow and give a five-minute view on how can we resolve the issue of a non-functioning Parliament time and again. What is your view on the issue? How does it compare with the rest of the world and what innovative solution can you think of? How should the government and the opposition work to ensure the Parliament works for development and yet remains fair and transparent? You can even make a slide presentation if you wish to.

I will live-tweet any good idea on my Twitter account so that 15 lakh people out there will follow your views.

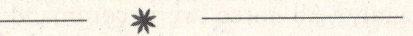

But then he started doubting his own idea and after a while he backtracked. 'But how can I ask them to give solutions when I don't have any myself?' For the next one hour we discussed option after option. We wanted to include this discussion in our upcoming book, *Advantage India*. One of the ideas that we were beginning to consider seriously was to have a settlement committee, which would consist of several referees. This committee could resolve any dispute that would stall the Parliament for more than five hours at a stretch. The committee would include the President, the Prime Minister, the leader of the Opposition and the Chief Justice of the Supreme Court. And we also decided that the hours lost during one parliamentary session must be added to the next session as overtime, so that the members of the Parliament can make up for the lost time.

The third instance was another beautiful display of his humility.

We were in a convoy of six to seven cars. Dr Kalam and I were in the second car. Ahead of us was a gypsy with an open back leading the convoy. In any convoy the leading car is called a 'pilot', as it controls the speed and direction of the entire fleet of vehicles behind it. In our pilot vehicle, there were three soldiers in the rear—two of them were sitting on either side and one lean guy was standing in the middle of the vehicle's open back. They were all holding their automatic guns tightly. All three were commandos wearing black scarves covering their faces. One hour into the road journey, Dr Kalam said, 'Why is he standing? He will get tired. This looks like a punishment for him. Can you send him a wireless message asking him to sit?' I said that maybe the commando had been instructed to keep standing for better security. But Dr Kalam would not relent. We tried radio-messaging the commando but that did not work. Probably due to the fierce wind blowing outside he could not hear what was being said. I looked at him, gesturing our inability to establish communication.

But he was resilient and in no mood to give up.

When the radio-messaging failed he decided to use hand signals. Alerted by the phone call, the soldiers in the lead pilot vehicles were already looking at us and they immediately picked up the hand signals, but with the wrong interpretation. They mistakenly thought that Dr Kalam was asking the pilot car to go faster so that the convoy could reach the destination earlier. Within no time they increased their speed and the entire convoy started speeding up on the mountainous road.

Our hand signals had clearly failed. But Dr Kalam still refused to give up.

He continued to wave his hand hoping that this time the soldiers in the pilot vehicle would understand what he meant. Again they misunderstood. When they saw him still waving his hand they thought that they they'd misread his signals and that Dr Kalam actually wanted to go slower. So then the convoy started losing speed and the cars started coming uncomfortably close thereby bumping into each other. Clearly, we were not able to get our message across.

Finally, realizing that there was little we could do at that moment, he told me, 'I want to meet this commando and thank him.' Later when we reached IIM Shillong, I went looking for the commando. But it was difficult to find him because all the commandos had their faces covered with black scarves and I had not seen his face. Moreover, all the guards were from local areas and there was a language barrier between us; they could not understand what I was saying. Finally after talking to three or four policemen and soldiers I managed to get hold of our man. But when I approached him he was confused.

Imagine being in his position. First, we'd radio-messaged him, then we'd sent him hand signals, and now Dr Kalam had sent his team to get him personally. He asked me timidly, 'Did I do something wrong?' I assured him that it was not the case.

I took him inside and Dr Kalam greeted him. He shook his hand and said, 'Thank you, buddy. Are you tired? I am sorry that you had to stand so long because of me. I was trying to ask you to sit down but I could not. I had AC in my car and a roof above my head but you were out in the open for hours. Sometimes life presents us with such difficulties. Now would you like something to eat?' He pointed to the person serving tea and biscuits. The young guard was surprised—he was, in fact, lost for words. Finally he said, *'Sir, aapke liye toh chhey ghante bhi khade rahenge.'* (I can keep standing for six hours to protect you.)

By then it was 6.25 p.m.

The lecture was about to start in five minutes. Dr Kalam insisted that we immediately head to the lecture hall where nearly two hundred students had assembled. The lecture hall was about five minutes away from the guest house that we were staying at. He did not want to be late for the lecture. 'A teacher should not make his students wait,' he'd always say.

I quickly set up his mic and briefed him on the final lecture, and while I was pinning his collar mic, he smiled and said, 'Funny guy, are you doing well?'

By 'funny guy' Dr Kalam could mean a variety of things. Depending on the tone and the occasion, it could mean you have done well, you have messed up, you should just listen to him, you have been plain naive, or he was just being jovial. Over the last six years I had learnt to interpret his 'funny guy's like the back of my hand. This was the last time I would be hearing this epithet.

I smiled back. 'Yes,' I replied. Those were the last words we said to each other. He began his lecture with a discussion on the conflicts existing amongst nations, especially between India and Pakistan. He completed his speech saying, 'I believe that when the youth all over the world come together for creating a better society and a better earth, then all the conflicts between nations will cease.'

There was a long pause. It was 6.40 p.m. on a chilly Shillong evening, and the last birds were returning to their nests. Their chirps were heard in the silence.

I thought that the screen that was showing him the vital points of the speech had gone blank and I looked up to see if I could resolve the problem. Just as I looked at him, his knees buckled and with a loud thud, he fell on the stage.

We rushed to pick him up. Before the doctors arrived, we tried whatever we could do to revive him. I will never forget the look in his half-closed eyes when I placed my hand on his head. I was desperately massaging his hands which were turning cold. His hands curled tightly over my fingers. His face had become still. His wise eyes were still radiating wisdom as they gradually became motionless. He never said a word. He did not show any pain—there was only peace on his face.

Within ten minutes we had taken him to the nearest hospital, Bethany. But in another few minutes the Missile Man had taken the eternal flight into the unknown. The doctors kept trying to make some miracle happen, but fate had passed its verdict. I touched his feet one last time. *Adieu old friend! Grand mentor, see you in my thoughts and meet you in the next life . . .*

I realized at that moment that he had actually departed doing what he loved the most—teaching. In his last moments he was standing tall and teaching, just the way he had wanted to. He left the world with no material deposits in his bank balance, but with huge deposits of wishes and love in his heart. He was successful till the end.

I will miss all the lunches and dinners that we had together, I will miss all the times that he surprised me with his humility and startled me with his curiosity, I will miss the lessons that he taught me with his actions, words and silence. I will miss the races to get into our flights in time, our trips and our long debates. He gave me dreams; he showed me that dreams need to be impossible because everything else is a compromise to my own ability. Above all I will remember that he moulded me into a better human being.

The man is gone, but the mission lives on.

* * *

The next morning at 4 a.m., when I was waiting in the Raj Bhavan, the phone rang continuously—people who loved him were calling to offer their condolences. But I had no energy to attend these calls. That was when I wrote something on social media to let the world know about Dr Kalam's last day.

Around 5 a.m. we flew in an Army helicopter to Guwahati. At 6 a.m., when we landed, there was a crowd of people mourning his death. My eyes particularly fell on a child of about ten who was clutching a picture that he had clicked with Dr Kalam four years ago. He was crying inconsolably. When I went to him he asked me, '*Wapis nahi ayenge?*' (Won't he come back?) I did not have the heart to tell him the truth. I just handed him the packet of fruit juice that someone had given me a few moments ago.

Later that day we brought his body back to Delhi where tens of thousands had assembled to see him for the last time and to pray for his soul. Till late in the night of the 28th people of all faiths came, praying in their own ways for the peace of his soul. Tears of sorrow were shed by eyes which had never seen him alive; hymns were sung in languages that he had never spoken in. Many groups of people stationed themselves outside his house and performed yajnas and poojas. The nation was weeping as one at the loss of their most beloved hero.

On the 29th, we took Dr Kalam to his hometown— Rameswaram. I had never visited the place before. I had once complained to him that he had never taken me there and he had replied, 'You fellow, come for my elder brother's birthday and stay there for a week.' I was now in Rameswaram but for a completely different event. Again a sea of people gathered at the island district. Amongst the ones who had come to pay him tribute was a policeman who had been his PSO during his visit to Kerala and a driver who had driven him in Mumbai. I wondered how they had managed to make this journey at such short notice. I am sure there were many other people in the gathering who had worked for him briefly, for a day or even less, who had protected him in convoys, or had driven his car—but his impact on them had been such that they had still come to bid him goodbye.

On the 30th, his mortal body was put to rest, a few feet beneath the earth. But his nobility, his enchanting ability to ignite hopes in despair, his humility and compassion and his sheer disregard for the impossible continue to live on and inspire generations ahead.

His story is far from over.

Where is our part in this story? It is in believing impossible dreams like Kalam. It is in trusting one's ability to change the world.

It is in living a life like Kalam.

It is in being a Kalam and always asking ourselves—

What can I give?

Epilogue

'Someday you will have to write a book on me,' Dr Kalam had said.

I had been startled, wondering whether I had heard him correctly. I mumbled, 'What?'

Sitting right across me, on the small lunch table at 10, Rajaji Marg, had been the beaming Dr A.P.J. Abdul Kalam. It had been the winter of 2011. I had already spent more than two years working with him and we were about to come out with our first book—*Target 3 Billion*.

'You should remember all these conversations. You may have to write a book about this. I wrote so much about my teachers—right from my primary-school teacher to my bosses, capturing the entire spectrum of six decades. Don't worry, you will manage it too.'

'Yes.' I hadn't been able to think of anything else to say right then.

Less than half a decade later, the book has been written.

Epilogue

The Kalam I knew was a great teacher. Great teachers never die, they never rust, they never fade. They just transform from mortal humans into immortal lessons—lessons carried over generations. This book is a tribute to my teacher and his lessons.

Read More

Reignited: *Scientific Pathways to a Brighter Future*
A. P. J. Abdul Kalam and Srijan Pal Singh

Will robots take over the world? When will we meet aliens? How are memories stored inside the brain?

Join Dr A.P.J. Kalam on a fascinating quest to explore the realm of science and technology, its extraordinary achievements and its impact on our lives in the days to come.

Co-written with Srijan Pal Singh, this book features exciting and cutting-edge career paths in areas such as robotics, aeronautics, neuroscience, pathology, palaeontology and material sciences . . . in other words, careers that are going to make a difference in the future. The result of extensive research, this book offers a plethora of ground-breaking ideas that will make youngsters think out of the box.

Filled with anecdotes, conversations, experiments and even inputs from leading scientists, *Reignited* is the perfect handbook that is bound to create a spark for science among students, youth and science enthusiasts.

Read More

My India: Ideas for the Future

Wisdom and inspiration from India's best-loved President!

My India: Ideas for the Future is a collection of excerpts from Dr A.P. J. Adbul Kalam's speeches in his post-presidency years. Drawn from Dr Kalam's addresses to parliaments, universities, schools and other institutions in India and abroad, they include his ideas on science, nation-building, poverty, compassion and self-confidence.

Dr Kalam draws on the lives of stalwarts such as Marie Curie and Dr Vikram Sarabhai to encourage and inspire his young readers. Through these speeches, he shares many valuable lessons in humility, resilience and determination, and leads children to think, grow and evolve.

A project very close to his heart, Dr Kalam's last book for children is a road map for every child to pursue their dreams, to be the best they can be, leading to the realization of a better India.